TEACHER'S GUIDE
with Dual-Purpose Duplicating Masters

BASIC JUDAISM FOR YOUNG PEOPLE
TORAH

LOIS MILLER COHN, M.S.

with Zev Jacobson

Foreword by Michael Zeldin, Ph.D.

This is the Teacher's Guide for Volume Two of *Basic Judaism for Young People,* by Naomi Pasachoff, Ph.D.

EDITORIAL BOARD

William Cutter, Rabbi, Ph.D., Chair
Elliot Dorff, Rabbi, Ph.D.
Gail Dorph, M.A.
Harold M. Schulweis, Rabbi, Th.D.
Michael Zeldin, Ph.D.

RESEARCH ASSOCIATE

Mordecai Finley, M.A.

BEHRMAN HOUSE, INC., PUBLISHERS
WEST ORANGE, NEW JERSEY

Copyright © 1987 by Behrman House, Inc.
235 Watchung Avenue
West Orange, New Jersey 07052

ISBN 0-87441-443-1

3 4 5 91

Designer: Betty Binns Graphics/Martin Lubin
Project Editor: Geoffrey Horn

CONTENTS

Things You Should Know About *Basic Judaism for Young People*		v
Foreword: Teaching *Basic Judaism for Young People*		iv
Preface: Teaching *Torah*		vx
1	Aggadah	1
2	Halachah	5
3	Haftarah	9
4	Ḥumash	13
5	Ketuvim	17
6	Leshon HaKodesh	21
7	Midrash	26
8	Mezuzah	31
9	Minhag	34
10	Mitzvah	39
11	Nevi'im	43
12	Sefer Torah	48
13	Aliyah	52
14	Aseret HaDibrot	55
15	Parashat HaShavua	59
16	Rashi	63
17	Torah	67
18	Talmud	73
19	Talmud Torah	77
20	Tanach	81

Dual-Purpose Duplicating Masters

1	Aggadah (Chapter 1)
2	Ḥumash (Chapter 4)
3	Ketuvim (Chapter 5)
4	Leshon HaKodesh (Chapter 6)
5	Mezuzah (Chapter 8)
6–7	Minhag (Chapter 9)
8–9	Nevi'im (Chapter 11)
10	Sefer Torah (Chapter 12)
11	Aliyah (Chapter 13)
12	Parashat HaShavua (Chapter 15)
13	Torah (Chapter 17)
14	Talmud (Chapter 18)
15	Talmud Torah (Chapter 19)
16A/B	Lesson Planning Form

THINGS YOU SHOULD KNOW ABOUT
BASIC JUDAISM FOR YOUNG PEOPLE

■ *Basic Judaism for Young People: Torah* is the second volume of a three-volume series. Associated Student Activity Books and Teacher's Guides make *Basic Judaism* a richly detailed course in Jewish ideas, practices, and values.

■ Each textbook volume consists of twenty chapters, arranged in Hebrew alphabetical order. Chapters may be taught in the original sequence or as one or more thematically organized mini-courses.

■ Each chapter begins with a Hebrew vocabulary-concept, its proper transliteration and pronunciation, and its formal definition. Each concept is then explored primarily through stories from the Biblical, rabbinic, and folk traditions.

■ Varied special topics, source notes, and visual aids supplement the main narrative.

■ Key terms and concepts appear in the text in Hebrew as well as English.

■ Each volume includes a glossary and index with extensive cross-references.

■ Each Student Activity Book and Teacher's Guide offers an abundance of activities for review, reinforcement, affective response, and creative expression.

■ All materials in the *Basic Judaism* series have been prepared under the supervision of an editorial board with extensive experience in contemporary Jewish education.

FOREWORD
TEACHING *BASIC JUDAISM* FOR YOUNG PEOPLE

What is the difference between these two moral lessons?

(1) Once there was a hyena. Like all hyenas, this one was greedy, but it had some reason to be because it had not eaten for several days. It ambled along the bush path desperate for food. The track divided. Which way should it go? The hyena hesitated. Then it lifted its head and sniffed to the right. Distant smells of food made its nostrils tingle. It began to move forward, then hesitated. Turning, it raised its head and sniffed at the air again, this time to the left. There was food in that direction too. What should the hyena do? It paused, turned right, hesitated and turned left, then right again like a disco dancer. It could not decide, until finally it tried to go in both directions at once, split itself in two and died."*

(2) Greed kills.

You might think the difference between the two anecdotes is obvious. One is a story, the other its moral; one amuses, the other preaches; one is long, the other short. But when we ask "What is the *educational* difference between these two?" then new answers emerge. One engages the intellect and the emotions, the other only the intellect; one is memorable, the other is not; one kindles the imagination, the other may not; one leads to a real understanding of the concept of greed, the other points out one characteristic of it.

Naomi Pasachoff's *Basic Judaism for Young People* introduces students to basic Jewish concepts in the engaging and educational language of the first of these two paragraphs—through the medium of stories. The stories Dr. Pasachoff tells about the sages of ancient Israel and the rabbis and leaders of the Jewish people since ancient times are the ideal teaching tool for reaching students of the intermediate grades (and, indeed, of any grade or age).

To begin with, stories entertain. Storytelling is as old as civilization and as contemporary as Hollywood. The narrative—the story with characters, plot, setting, and mood—is the perfect way to capture students' attention and keep them involved and engaged.

Second, stories are memorable because they capture the imagination. One quick reference to a well-known story can set off a chain reaction within us. The magical

---

*Quoted from "Concepts with Blurred Edges: Story and the Religious Imagination" by Jack G. Priestley in *Religious Education* 78:3 (Summer 1983): 377–89. The analysis is my own.

words *Cinderella, Pinocchio, The Boy Who Cried Wolf,* or *E.T.* bring to mind a flood of associations, often accompanied by an equally strong flood of emotions.

Third, stories are rich sources of ideas. A good story can be read (or heard) over and over again. Each time the reader can find new meaning, learn new lessons, or gain new insights. A group of readers reading together can share and exchange ideas, enriching each other's understanding.

Finally, stories can convey ethical truths and human insights much more effectively than merely stating the moral. In the hyena story,

> the simple statement "greed kills" may sum up the moral point of the story but that is all it does do. What it does not do is to forge a link between knowing and acting. Analysis not only breaks the story down. It also separates the intellectual from the affective, the moral concept from the moral action.... If the story has been well told I have absorbed the knowledge that greed kills not just through my detached intellect but within the context of real hunger pains. I have entered the situation in which I might really be tempted to be greedy. I have faced the moral dilemma contained in my own emotional reactions when standing hungrily at the crossroads and I have resolved it, in this case, catastrophically, for I have *been* the hyena, felt his hunger, experienced his greed, known his inner state of mind and have been destroyed.... And the process has been one of imagination ... (Priestley, p. 384).

The stories of *Basic Judaism for Young People* thus provide students with a wealth of imaginative, entertaining experiences through which they can come to understand Jewish ideas and values. Each of the three books—*Israel, Torah,* and *God*—is organized around twenty such ideas, presented in the form of a basic Jewish vocabulary item.

Basic Jewish Vocabulary

Some scholars believe the key to understanding a culture is understanding the vocabulary it uses to describe the world. The oft-repeated example that Eskimos have dozens of words for snow makes the point well. To an Eskimo, whose environment is snow, distinctions among types of snow are essential, but to an outsider (especially one from a temperate climate), snow is snow. Since outsiders don't have the vocabulary to describe different kinds of snow, they may not even notice the distinctions. Possession of a rich vocabulary is important not only because it aids in communication but also because, in its absence, certain thoughts are literally unthinkable.

Just as many Eskimo words for snow have no adequate English equivalents, many Jewish concepts are not fully expressed by simple English translations. The English terms may be close, but they do not really permit the English speaker to grasp the subtleties of the Jewish culture and value system. Here is where the stories in *Basic Judaism for Young People* make their most profound contribution. The stories provide the rich associations and deeper understandings that simple translations alone cannot provide.

For a young person to live in a Jewish environment and participate in Jewish culture, familiarity with the vocabulary of Judaism is essential. A Jewish vocabulary enables a Jew to think like a Jew, feel like a Jew, and act like a Jew. This vocabulary allows the Jew to enter the world of Jews of old and to communicate meaningfully with other Jews living today. Such a vocabulary allows the Jew to share in and contribute to the rich cultural heritage of the Jewish people.

Planning the Course

While the textbook can form the backbone of your curriculum for a year-long course on basic Jewish concepts and ideas, only your creativity in matching elements of the textbook to the needs of the class and school can make the course a success. In order to breathe more life into the printed page, you must combine intuition with systematic planning to prepare lessons and units that are involving, exciting, and appropriate to both the learners and the subject matter. Then, as you transform your plans into a living lesson, flexibility should be your hallmark as you follow awakening student interests while keeping in mind the target concepts.

The chapters of *Basic Judaism for Young People* are arranged in Hebrew alphabetical order. By going through the chapters in sequence, you can develop a course with great variety, teaching a different theme related to a different concept each week. Thus your course would move from particularistic to universalistic themes and back again; from individual to communal values and back again; and from the ancient to the modern world and back again. This organizational plan has two advantages: it proves for diversity, and it allows for periodic review of related themes at different times during the year.

However, there is no reason why the book must be taught in the order presented. Later chapters do on occasion refer to stories and characters mentioned earlier in the book, but these are often passing references rather than essential steps in a cumulative learning process. Thus, the textbook allows you the freedom and flexibility to organize your course in any number of different ways, depending on your own values and interests and the needs of your students and school.

The concepts presented in the textbook can be used to explore a variety of themes in Jewish life, and you can select chapters and arrange them in a sequence that allows you to expand on the themes you feel are appropriate. Also, since there may be more material than you are able to cover adequately during the school year, you can select concepts you feel are the most important rather than just skipping the last chapters of the book.

Several possible themes for units, together with the appropriate chapters, are suggested below. You can select themes, organize them in any order you see fit, and then choose the concepts (i.e., chapters in *Basic Judaism for Young People*) to teach as part of the exploration of those themes.

Planning Lessons

The planning procedure outlined below is not intended as a recipe to be followed precisely, but rather as a series of suggestions designed to spark your own creative flair. It is a systematic procedure, but a good mix of creativity and intuition can enhance the process and yield dynamic and educationally sound lessons. The steps in the suggested planning process are:

(1) What is it?—Thinking through the concept;
(2) What will students get out of it?—Setting objectives and outcomes;
(3) What to do?—Developing activities;
(4) Do they get it?—Planning for reading and comprehension;
(5) What's first?—Deciding how to begin;
(6) What's last?—Deciding how to conclude.

You should note that each chapter in *Basic Judaism for Young People* is divided into two or three lessons. Given a significant block of time (at least one and one-half hours), you may be able to include an entire chapter in a single class session. Otherwise, each lesson in the textbook should occupy a single classroom period (from 40 to 60 minutes). If you are dividing a chapter into several class sessions, you will have to make provision at the beginning of the second session to review the material covered in the first session and to make a transition to the material to be covered in the second session. However, the two sessions should be treated as a single unit that explores different facets of one concept. Review and reinforcement at the end of the second session should take this into account.

(1) What is it?—Thinking through the concept The first step in planning lessons using *Basic Judaism for Young People* is to consider the meaning of the concepts presented in the textbook chapter. Jewish concepts are usually multifaceted, and while the textbook introduces concepts to children on their level, you should enter the classroom with a more thorough understanding.

In particular, you should be careful not to confuse Jewish concepts with their English translations. One of the aims of the textbook is to introduce students to the basic conceptual vocabulary of Judaism and thus help them develop a Jewish way of thinking. Distinctions between Hebrew concepts and their English translations become quite important in this process. "Tzedakah" provides a case in point. This term is normally translated into English as "charity." Yet as the definition in the *Israel* volume points out, Tzedakah and charity are not synonymous, even though both usually involve the giving of money to someone in need. Charity is an act of benevolence or good will, while Tzedakah conveys both a sense of obligation on the part of the giver and the implication that the reason for helping another is that it is the just and fair thing to do. Thus, the key question that should guide you as you begin your own exploration of each concept is, "How is the Jewish concept like its English translation, and how is it different?"

A second step in thinking through the concept is to think of appropriate examples. Giving money to a friend so he or she can buy a new toy is *not* an example of Tzedakah (although it may, under certain circumstances, be an instance of Raḥamanut), but giving toys to an orphanage *is* an example of Tzedakah.

The third and final step in thinking through a concept is to outline the features of that concept. You should pay particular attention to features that are addressed in the textbook—in the definition, in the introductory text, or in the stories. For example, the features of Tzedakah highlighted in the *Israel* textbook are:

- Tzedakah is a duty.
- Tzedakah often involves giving money.
- Tzedakah helps the needy.
- The giver of Tzedakah benefits in many intangible ways.
- Giving Tzedakah is an obligation for everyone.

Armed with a rich understanding of the concept on an adult level, you are ready to plan to teach the concept to children. You can then provide your students a clear and consistent understanding of the concept and can respond to students' questions and comments that go beyond the material explicitly stated in the textbook. This Teacher's Guide is designed to provide you with some additional information about and a deeper understanding of the concepts presented in the textbook.

(2) What will students get out of it?—Setting objectives and outcomes Once you understand the concept, you will want to decide what you want students to "get" out of the class lessons. You may want to state these in terms of both *performance objectives* and *expressive outcomes*. Performance objectives specify in very precise terms what you want students to be able to do at the end of the lessons that they cannot do at the beginning. Performance objectives consist of the phrase "By the end of the lesson students will be able to . . ." followed by an active verb and a content. "Identify," "list," "restate in their own words," and "give an example" are expressions frequently used to identify basic abilities that students can master within the span of a single class session. Other expressions can—and should—be used to state objectives for higher-level thinking skills: for example, "analyze," "indicate the reasons for," "predict," and "express agreement or disagreement with."

Unlike performance objectives, expressive outcomes do not identify specific behaviors that result from learning. Instead, they indicate students' possible reactions to the learning process. They are "the consequences of curriculum activities that are intentionally planned to provide a fertile field for personal purposing and experience."* Thinking about expressive outcomes allows us to concern ourselves not only with the end-products of each lesson but also with the ongoing experiences of children as they learn.

Expressive outcomes acknowledge the individuality of each learner. Rather than specifying a common objective for all children, expressive outcomes recognize the likelihood that different children will have different reactions to their learning experiences. Often expressed as opportunities provided to students, such outcomes frequently emphasize affective (i.e., emotional and identity-related) issues.

(3) What to do?—Developing activities After you understand the concept and have determined what you want the lesson to accomplish, you may want to turn your lesson planning directly to the major learning activities. The purpose of the major activities should be to extend and reinforce the students' comprehension of each chapter. Activities should fit the objectives and outcomes and should provide students with the opportunity to:

- review the stories in the text in a new and different way;
- think about the concepts in the text in new situations;
- apply the concepts in the text to contemporary life;
- make decisions about the applicability and relevance of the concepts in the text; and/or
- develop original ways to present the concepts or stories to others.

Along with the actual reading of the textbook, the major activities form the cornerstone of the lesson, in terms of time, emphasis, and potential benefit. As you select, design, and prepare these activities, you should strive for variety and for harmony with your specified objectives and outcomes. Student Activity Book exercises that call on students to personalize the concepts can often be incorporated into these activities.

(4) Do they get it?—Planning for reading and comprehension The single most important challenge you face is helping students enjoy reading the text and understanding its im-

---

*The notion of expressive outcomes is explained by Elliot W. Eisner in *The Educational Imagination* (New York: Macmillan, 1979).

portant points. You will therefore not want to neglect planning this part of the lesson as carefully as you plan other parts. Among the reading techniques you may find useful are:

- having different students read as others follow along;
- reading yourself while students follow along;
- reading to the students without having them follow the text;
- reading the story yourself beforehand and retelling the story in your own words;
- reading or telling the story to the students, then having them read it silently or aloud;
- having different students take different roles, especially for stories with substantial dialogue.

Whichever method you use for any given lesson (and you may want to use a different technique each time), you should consider interrupting the reading at various points in order to do the following:

- Look at and discuss pictures and illustrations, especially as they are referred to in the text.
- Have a short discussion about questions in the text that are directed at students.
- Check for understanding of difficult words, phrases, and ideas by asking simple questions.
- Review the plot of the story, either halfway through or just before the "climax," by asking students to retell the story in their own words.
- Emphasize important points in the story by asking leading questions designed to check for comprehension of ideas.
- Look at the "Have You Heard?" "What Time Is It?" and/or "See for Yourself" sections of the chapter. They set the context for the story, provide enrichment information, and can be helpful in increasing students' understanding.

Note that at this stage you want to focus on students' understanding of the story. You will probably want to confine your questions to those which check on understanding, rather than moving to the more complex areas of analysis or opinion. Immediately following the reading of the story, you may want to have students turn to the comprehension exercises in the Student Activity Book and only then move on to the major activities of the lesson.

(5) What's first?—Deciding how to begin Only after you have planned the lesson can you decide how to begin it. You may want to keep in mind that at the very beginning of class you will want to accomplish three things:

(**1**) capture students' interest;

(**2**) make them feel comfortable in class by using what they already know;

(**3**) point toward the content of the lesson.

The chapters and lessons in the textbook often have built-in beginnings that can accomplish all three of these purposes. These beginnings usually either ask students an open-ended question about their own experiences or focus on a photograph or illustration in the textbook. If you want to use a chapter or lesson introduction as a beginning to your class session, you should do it conversationally rather than reading from the text. You might, for example, pose the question asked in the text to begin a short class discussion and only afterward have students turn directly to the chapter. Or you might have students look at an illustration in the chapter and ask them questions designed to elicit the information given in the text. Actually reading the textbook then serves to review and reinforce the introductory discussion. Additional suggestions for beginnings are given in each chapter of this Teacher's Guide, but you will, of course, want to use your own creativity and your knowledge of your students to decide how to begin each class session.

(6) What's last?—Deciding how to conclude The last planning decision you will have to make is deciding how to conclude the class session. The conclusion may serve one of several purposes:

- review the lesson;
- reinforce the content of the lesson;
- provide a transition to the next lesson;
- pose questions for further thought;
- elicit individual reactions to the lesson;
- evaluate how successfully the objectives and outcomes have been achieved.

This is a particularly good time to turn to the "Review It" sections of the textbook. They provide a variety of questions ranging from simple review of the story to complex extensions of the concepts to new situations.

By following this planning procedure, you will be able to develop lesson plans that are well thought out, provide a variety of learning activities, alllow for imaginative thinking, and offer excitement and involvement for you and your students. To help you in your planning, especially at the beginning of the year, a lesson-planning form is provided as Dual-Purpose Duplicating Masters #16 A/B. You can run them off "back-to-back" and use them as you plan each chapter. Space is provided at the bottom for you to write down your reactions after teaching, either for your own future reference or for submission to the principal.

Special Features of the Textbook

As you leaf through the textbook, you will no doubt notice several special sections that accompany the main narrative and illustrations. You should not overlook them; they can give you many opportunities for teaching and enrichment.

Definitions Each chapter begins with a definition of the concept discussed in that chapter. Usually the definition is accompanied by a literal translation of the Hebrew. Remember that although it is important for students to read and understand the definition, knowing the definition is only a first step toward understanding the full meaning of the concept.

Have You Heard? These short marginal notes provide background for the story or supply enrichment information. Depending on your students' level of understanding and your own preference, you may choose to have the whole class read these notes together, or you may suggest them as additional reading for more able students.

What Time Is It? Several time-lines set the stories and their events and characters in historical perspective. While *Basic Judaism for Young People* is not a history textbook per se, it can be useful in helping students understand the basic periods of the Jewish past. The stories in the text are taken from the Biblical, rabbinic, medieval, and modern periods. In the text, the stories skip around from era to era, since they were selected for the light they shed on Jewish concepts, not for what they teach about Jewish history. Even though the teaching of historical details is not a goal of this textbook, you may want to use the time-lines to help students see how much the Jewish past contributes to today's understanding of Judaism.

See for Yourself These marginal notes refer students and teachers to the Biblical and/or Talmudic sources mentioned in the stories. The Bible, as the cornerstone of the Jewish tradition, has been the basis for most later developments in Jewish life. The rabbis and the medieval commentators referred to the Bible constantly, for they felt it contained all the answers to life's questions. In modern times, Jews have frequently looked to the Bible as a source—if not the last word—on many Jewish and universal issues. "See for Yourself" directs you to the exact verses in the Bible or sections of the Babylonian Talmud that either figure in or serve as the basis for the stories. Looking at the Biblical references in a modern Jewish translation (such as the new Jewish Publication Society edition of the Tanach) can enrich your own and your more advanced students' understanding.

Glossary While the concepts in the textbook are arranged in alef-bet order, you may sometimes want to get a quick definition of a term without having to figure out the Hebrew sequence. The Glossary provides a handy cross-reference arranged in English alphabetical order. You will notice that Hebrew and Yiddish terms used in the text are included here even if they are not chapter headings. The Glossary should be the first place you look if you or your students come across an unfamiliar word.

A Note to Teachers: The Teachable Moment

The most effective teaching of concepts and values grows out of real-life situations. An argument on the playground, a disagreement in class, a guest or a new child in school, an event in the life of one of the students—all these provide "teachable moments" at which children are particularly receptive to new ideas and new values.

When you are teaching with *Basic Judaism for Young People*, you should be particularly alert for these "teachable moments" as they occur during the school day. Opportunities for teaching Shalom may come as a result of a classroom fight; you may be able to teach Raḥamanut when a sensitive moment in the life of one of the children arises; or you may have the chance to discuss Kevod HaBriot when children come in contact with special education students. A quick mention of a concept at one of these times—or a short (five-minute) discussion of the applicability of a concept already studied—can often make a more lasting impression than a full hour of formal teaching. If you can lead students to see the connections between what they are studying and the situations they encounter daily, the educational benefits can be enormous. The rewards may be even greater if you induce the students to make such connections through skillful questioning and discussion leading, rather than by pointing them out yourself.

So be on the lookout for "teachable moments"!

A Special Note to Day School Teachers

Basic Judaism for Young People can be used in day schools, especially those with an "integrated" curriculum, by either the general studies or the Hebrew/Judaica teacher. The textbook provides a bridge between Jewish concepts and English language skills. It is an excellent source for the teaching of literature, reading skills, and values. It can also be a helpful source for reinforcing concepts taught in the school's Judaica program or as a way to infuse the teaching of Jewish values into the school's secular program.

Basic Judaism for Young People can form the basis for a year-long Judaica curriculum if you follow the basic outline presented in this Teacher's Guide but adapt it to the rhythms of the day school. More Hebrew can be used, concepts can be reviewed more frequently, and the values can be explored from many more angles than is possible when less time is available. Alternatively, the textbook can be a supplement in the reading/language arts program, used intermittently to introduce Jewish concepts or to reinforce reading or language arts skills. It can also be used extensively in the teaching of literature. *Basic Judaism for Young People* offers many examples of short stories and folk tales, and suggestions for teaching these genres are interspersed throughout this Teacher's Guide.

Whether you use the textbook in the Judaica curriculum or the general studies program, it can enhance students' knowledge and awareness of their Jewish heritage. By adapting the suggestions in this Teacher's Guide, the day school teacher can help bridge the gap between Jewish culture and general culture by helping students develop a deeper understanding of the concepts and values of Judaism.

MICHAEL ZELDIN

PREFACE
TEACHING TORAH

Basic Judaism for Young People: Torah can be taught as a sequence of twenty concepts arranged in Hebrew alphabetical order. However, the text can also be taught as one or more mini-courses.

Sample Thematic Units

The Hebrew Bible
Ḥumash
Ketuvim
Nevi'im
Tanach

Other Sources of Jewish Knowledge
*Aggadah
*Halachah
*Midrash
*Minhag
Torah
Talmud
Talmud Torah

Law and Custom
*Halachah
*Minhag
Mitzvah
Aseret HaDibrot

Language and Literature
*Aggadah
Leshon HaKodesh
*Midrash
Rashi

Ritual and Practice
Haftarah
Mezuzah
*Minhag
Sefer Torah
Aliyah
Parashat HaShavua

*Concepts marked with an asterisk can be used in more than one thematic unit.

Using This Teacher's Guide

This Teacher's Guide for *Basic Judaism for Young People: Torah* consists of twenty chapters (corresponding to the twenty chapters in the textbook), followed by a series of dual-purpose duplicating masters. A list of masters follows the Table of Contents. Each chapter has seven main headings: *Objectives, Background, Words to the Wise, Delving into the Chapter, Up for Discussion, Write On!,* and *And Finally.* . . .

Objectives The list of numbered objectives corresponds to the "performance objectives" discussed in the Foreword by Michael Zeldin. You may want to use all or some of them in connection with the lesson planning form (Duplicating Masters #16A/B).

Background This section is intended to broaden your knowledge of the concept discussed in the chapter. You should not try to impart this material to your students directly; rather, you should read the section before planning the lesson, in order to clarify your own thoughts, feelings, and values. Occasionally, the section will suggest additional readings to help you augment your understanding of the concept and help you deal with questions that students may raise.

Words to the Wise Listed in this section are the key terms in the chapter, as well as certain other terms and phrases your students may find difficult to comprehend. An asterisk next to a term indicates that its definition appears in the Glossary (textbook, pp. 146–48). Hebrew is given next to the English only when the Hebrew actually appears in the chapter.

Vocabulary study forms an important part of *Basic Judaism for Young People: Torah*. For each chapter, students should be able to recall the key concept (in Hebrew as well as English characters), its conventional English translation, its distinctively Jewish associations, and at least one story linked to it in the text.

Vocabulary study can become part of your regular classroom activity through:
- flash cards;
- spelling or defining "bees," based on either English or Hebrew;
- "What am I?" questions;
- matching questions that list Hebrew terms and their possible definitions;
- lookup exercises in the text Glossary or a Jewish encyclopedia;
- having students use key words in original sentences or make up their own stories about them.

Delving into the Chapter This section, which correspnds with "Beginning the Lesson" on the lesson planning form, generally includes a series of leading questions or guided activities designed to introduce your students to the material and raise issues that will be discussed more fully later.

Up for Discussion We have tried to provide an ample variety of stimulating ideas for open-ended discussion. Some of the starters are directly based on the text; others involve "what if" assumptions or role playing.

Write On! Writing provides an opportunity for students to explore their own thoughts and feelings and for you to assess how well they have assimilated the material in the chapter. Writing assignments range from factual research reports to personal narratives and creative flights of fancy. Try to provide an environment in which your students think of writing as fun—not as "busy work" or as punishment for misbehavior. Whenever possible, encourage your students to read, listen, and learn from other students' writing.

And Finally . . . This concluding section indicates the appropriate review and reinforcement exercises in the Student Activity Book. The section also suggests which chapters would make an effective followup; such suggestions may be used in connection with the sample thematic units listed earlier. Lastly, the section lists answers to factual questions raised in the text ("Review It"), the Student Activity Book, and the duplicating masters.

Breaking the Ice

Cooperative exercises are always a good way to break down barriers between teachers and students, so that an honest exchange of opinions can take place. The Teacher's Guide offers a number of food-related group activities, including a co-op salad, latkes, bimuelos, and Ḥanukkah cookies.

The introductory exercise in the Student Activity Book (p. 1) can be an excellent way for you to get to know your students' interests and for them to learn about each other. You might also want to make an "island," so that your students can learn a little about you.

Since the theme of the Introduction (text, pp. 1–2) is the relation between Torah, truth, and the alef-bet, a cooperative activity centered around the Hebrew alphabet might also be an excellent way to get the semester off to a good start. A patchwork tapestry is an easy, attractive way to display the alef-bet in your classroom. For this exercise you'll need:

Lightweight cardboard or tag board cut into 12" × 12" squares

Crayons or felt-tip markers

Paper hole punch

Colored yarn

Depending on class size, each student will be responsible for decorating one or more squares. Each square should have a large Hebrew letter in the center, surrounded by a colorful decorative pattern. Lay out the alef-bet squares in the correct sequence, leaving the four corners of the tapesty for designs and/or the students' names. Punch holes an inch apart on the inner edges of the squares; lace the squares together with yarn, making sure to pull the yarn so that the squares fit together tightly. The class can decorate the entire tapestry with fringes or tassels. Your students can then share the tapestry with a class just learning the alef-bet, display their handiwork in the synagogue or social hall, or keep the tapestry as a classroom decoration.

CHAPTER ONE

AGGADAH

Objectives

1. To introduce the concept of Aggadah as stories from classical Jewish literature.

2. To distinguish Aggadah from Halachah by showing the different literary purposes they serve and the different values they express.

3. To demonstrate how Aggadah helps us deal with such difficult questions as the powers of God and the meaning of life and death.

Background

Aggadah, the portion of rabbinic teaching that is *not* Halachah, developed as a way of presenting great moral and ethical values through stories, parables, and maxims. Aggadah and Halachah—laws and regulations for Jewish observance—together make up the Talmud.

The text does not define Aggadah in so formal a manner. Instead, the chapter emphasizes the way that Aggadah can touch the heart of the average Jew—the person who finds high intellectual concepts remote. The purpose of Aggadah was to bring issues down to the level of popular understanding, while raising the people's level of understanding to a higher plane. The storytellers' intent was not to create works of art (although works of art were indeed created) but to aid and instruct the people.

The Talmud is not a legal brief, and its editors felt no compulsion to smooth out all inconsistencies and contradictions. Sometimes Aggadot are meant as goads to a new way of thinking; sometimes they are meant as a challenge to prevailing notions. Often their effect is to "stretch" the listener or reader.

There is no single way of interpreting an Aggadah. Interpretations of Aggadah may be as varied as the number of people hearing them. For an exercise showing how one scene can evoke many different responses, see the duplicating master for this chapter.

Make sure your students understand the difference between *Aggadah* and *Haggadah*. Both terms come from the word meaning "to tell." However, when we speak of "Aggadot" we usually mean stories from classical Jewish literature, and when we say "Haggadah" we mean a particular book that is read at the Passover seder.

Words to the Wise

Key terms:

*Aggadah (אַגָּדָה)

*Halachah

Havdalah

rabban

Sanhedrin

sermon

Other terms:

console

goblet

mourning

*Definition appears in text Glossary. See the introduction to this Teacher's Guide for ways to make vocabulary study a classroom activity.

Delving into the Chapter

Go over with the class the definition of Aggadah that appears in the textbook on p. 3. Ask your students briefly to retell any fairy tales or fables that were read or told to them. What lessons or morals did they contain?

Remind your students that stories of this kind have lasted through the years because they are enjoyable and because they contain kernels of truth that help us understand our own lives and those of our ancestors. Discuss the fact that many fables and folk tales began as part of an oral tradition—they were told aloud and passed down by word of mouth from generation to generation.

Have your students read the story of Rabbi Abbahu and Rabbi Ḥiyya. Ask for interpretations and compare the various responses. You might ask:

- Does the expression "Just a spoonful of sugar makes the medicine go down" have any application here?
- Which type of sermon is more interesting to you?
- Is Halachah more important than Aggadah?

Develop these themes by having students complete pp. 5–7 of the Student Activity Book. Then have students read the stories of Rabbi Joshua and Rabban Gamaliel. Use the "Review It" questions in the textbook (p. 7) as the basis for classroom discussion.

The Aggadah about mourning tackles a very difficult subject and could be the basis of extended classroom discussion. You and your students may well find this homily unsatisfactory: can anyone really be consoled in such painful circumstances?

Expand the question "Why did Beruriah tell her husband she had to return a borrowed treasure from its owner?"

- How do you think this Aggadah explains the meaning of life? Or does it?
- Do you think Beruriah eased her husband's pain?
- What would have been the difference if she had just come right out and told him their sons were dead?

- Would he have felt any better or worse?
- What does this story tell you about Beruriah's relationship with her husband?
- What kind of woman do you think she was?
- What did Beruriah mean when she said "They went for a visit and have now returned"?

Up for Discussion

1. Challenge the class with the following question: What's the difference between the expressions "God is everywhere" and "God is everywhere we look for Him"?

2. An Aggadah just might be able to bring together groups who are at odds with each other, or at least help each group to understand the other's point of view. How might an Aggadah help parents understand the popularity of pop music, a current fad or philosophy, a strange new movie, etc.? Could an Aggadah help Palestinian Arabs better understand the viewpoint of Israeli Jews (or vice versa), or an American president better understand the attitudes of a Soviet leader (or vice versa)? Have small groups of students devise such Aggadot and tell them to the rest of the class.

3. *Ask the rabbi.* Invite the rabbi in for an interview or "press conference." Students might be encouraged to ask:

- How do you choose the topics for your sermons?
- What steps do you follow in writing your sermons?
- Do you ever have any problems when writing a sermon?
- Do you follow the approach of Rabbi Abbahu or of Rabbi Ḥiyya, or do you use a mixture of both?
- How do you make use of Aggadah and Halachah in your sermons?

Write On!

1. The story of George Washington and the cherry tree is a tale that may or may not be true but that illustrates his honesty. Have each student write an Aggadah about a favorite famous person that illustrates a well-known character trait (e.g., the faith of Abraham, the courage of Esther, the brilliance of Einstein).

2. Have students choose one of the following topics and write a short sermon to present to the class:

- A Good Story Helps in a Tough Situation
- Tzedakah: A True Story
- Where Is God?
- Aggadah Is for the Many, Halachah Is for the Few

Ask students to follow the techniques either of Rabbi Abbahu or Rabbi Ḥiyya. Have the sermons read aloud to the class and see whether the "congregation" can tell which sermons emphasize practice (Halachah) and which stress beliefs, ideas, and values (Aggadah).

3. The third question in the "Review It" on p. 8 would be a good written exercise. Look for some of the following responses:
- Some difficult questions have no absolute answer.
- There can be many sides to a story.
- A story may balance the many aspects of an issue.
- A story makes the answer easier to understand.

And Finally ...

See how well the class does on "Take Five" (Student Activity Book, p. 9).

NOTE: The next chapter, "Halachah" (text, pp. 9–14), is an obvious followup. Alternatively, this would be a good time to introduce the Midrash chapter (text, pp. 45–52). While Aggadah and Midrash are both concerned with storytelling, Midrash is a more technical term and constitutes a specific genre. Coupling the two chapters provides some interesting contrasts and similarities.

Answers to "Review It" Questions: p. 7: (1) the Aggadah about sunlight; (2) the Aggadah about the silver and golden goblets; p. 8: (1) c.

Answers to Student Activity Book Questions: p. 5: all אֱמֶת *except* (2) Aggadah, (3) Halachah, (7) Aggadah, (8) including, (9) Aggadah; p. 9: (1) "narration" or "telling a story"; (2) text gives the power of God and the meaning of life and death.

Answers to Duplicating Master #1: (a) 5, (b) 3, (c) 6, (d) 1, (e) 7, (f) 4, (g) 2.

CHAPTER TWO

HALACHAH

Objectives

1. To introduce the concept of Halachah as Jewish law.

2. To indicate the normative role Halachah plays in Jewish life.

3. To show that Halachah, although rooted in the Torah, changes as the conditions of Jewish life change.

4. To demonstrate that Halachah must be determined by majority opinion of qualified Jewish scholars.

Background

The term "Halachah" can be narrowly defined, in contradistinction to Aggadah, as the legal material in the Talmud. More broadly, Halachah is the entire legal system of Judaism, embracing the Written Law (the Five Books of Moses); the Oral Law, which consists of interpretations of the Written Law; and the responsa, which represent interpretations, clarifications, and adaptations of prior law to fit the changing circumstances of Jewish life.

Members of the American Jewish community hold differing views on Halachah—how much authority it should have and where that authority comes from. Some communities regard the civil laws of the Talmud and responsa as binding, while other communities believe that only Jewish ritual matters are governed by Halachah. In your classroom, you are likely to have students whose families treat Halachah in many different ways. Without confusing your students, you can point out the two extremes to be avoided: on the one hand, the belief that Halachah may be made up as we go along, or disregarded entirely; on the other hand, the belief that Halachah is embodied solely in a few venerable texts and is not at all open to change or challenge in our own time.

Halachah is a dynamic issue in Jewish life, and, accordingly, there is a twofold thrust to the chapter. The text recognizes that Jewish practice has been modernized throughout the ages and that Halachah continues to change today. Nevertheless, the chapter also recognizes that Halachah is the foundation of Jewish behavior and the core of what makes Judaism unique. Halachah is a link from generation to generation and from community to community. Changes in Halachah should not be taken lightly.

Words to the Wise

Key terms:

*Aggadah

B.C.E.

C.E.

*Halachah (הֲלָכָה)

Other terms:

anointing

carob

democratically

distinctive

interpretation

observance

Delving into the Chapter

Read and discuss with your students the introductory definition (text, p. 9), which points out that Halachah is the distinctive core of Judaism and that it is constantly changing. The importance of change is reinforced by the exercise on p. 10 of the Student Activity Book. After the activity has been completed, ask for volunteers to share their responses. Record the responses on the chalkboard using a format similar to that of the book. After comparing responses, ask the class:

- Why should rules and practices change for you as you grow older? (Answers should include comments about growing responsibility and changing needs, tastes, and abilities.)
- How did you and your parents decide when it was time for some change or reinterpretation of your personal "Halachah"?

The story about the crowns may puzzle some of your students. You can guide the discussion by asking:

- According to the story, why did God put crowns on some of the letters of the Torah?
- How did this special way of writing the Torah letters help Akiba understand where the Halachah had come from?
- Why was Moses unable to understand Rabbi Akiba's interpretation?
- Why was Moses pleased by what he witnessed?

Continue with the section on the details of observance. Explain the fact that Orthodox Jews follow very literally the Yom Kippur Halachot for eating, washing, anointing, and not wearing leather shoes. The Orthodox observe these Yom Kippur laws with all the care one devotes to laws that forbid stealing from or injuring another person. The importance of law in society and in Judaism is reinforced by the activity on p. 12 of the Student Activity Book.

"If there were no laws to guide the Jewish people, would there still be a Jewish people?" Jews all over the world, for example, know exactly what to do on Passover. Even though specific customs may vary (see the "Minhag" chapter, pp. 61–66 of the text), everyone knows what foods are required, and what order to follow in the seder. A Jew from Norway or Italy who came to your house during a seder would certainly know what was going on.

Remind your students that they are all from different homes, yet they all function together as a group. What holds the class together? (Someone will surely say "our rules" or something to that effect.) Ask your students to list classroom rules on the chalkboard—these may include rules of conduct, homework, etc. Ask if there are any that could be interpreted in more than one way. For example, is "No talking during class time" an absolute? What about during group meetings or class discussions? Positive rules like "Respect the rights of others" or "Make learning fun" could be subjected to similar analysis. Finally, ask the class what would happen if there were no rules at all.

A reading or dramatization of the debate between Rabbi Eliezer and the other rabbis can serve as a springboard for a discussion on compromise. Try to draw examples of compromise from the students' own experience.

- Suppose you want to stay at a friend's house until ten at night. Your parents want you home by seven. What compromise could be worked out so that everyone would be happy?

- Perhaps you want to spend Sunday afternoon at an arcade and your best friend wants to go to a movie. How would you work that one out?

Extend the discussion by considering a point of disagreement in contemporary Judaism. For example, the Orthodox are not allowed to drive to synagogue on Shabbat and other holidays, but Reform Jews do this freely and most Conservative Jews do so as well.

- Can students use the principle of compromise in order to create a new Halachah for Shabbat driving?

- In order to make this decision, what authorities and texts would the students want to consult?

- Should the final decision be approved by majority vote? If so, should this majority include everyone or just those who have studied the question closely?

See p. 11 of the Student Activity Book for an exercise to reinforce the concepts of interpretation and majority rule in determining Halachah.

Up for Discussion

1. "Every generation has its own truth...." Challenge your students to say whether this idea helps or hinders good relationships between parents and children. Make sure the students support their answers.

2. What are some "truths" your students believe in, but that their parents may not necessarily agree with? (Curfew, tastes in clothing, music, etc.) How does each family resolve such differences?

3. What are some things your students like now that they did not like before? Conversely, can your students give examples of things they *dislike* now that once were favorites? What accounts for these changes? You should feel free to share some of your own changing likes and dislikes with the class.

Write On!

1. Have students describe some of the activities that Jews refrain from on Yom Kippur. What positive steps toward self-improvement do Jews take on that day? Students can draw pictures illustrating what they do on Yom Kippur. (Prepare a bulletin board to display their work.)

2. "You shall love your neighbor as yourself" (Leviticus 19:18). Have students write an interpretation of this famous commandment. Does it mean that everything you have you should share with your neighbor? Does the word "neighbor" include family and friends? Suppose someone used this commandment to justify sharing test answers with a person sitting nearby—would *that* be a proper interpretation?

And Finally ...

"Take Five" (Student Activity Book, p. 13).

NOTE: Instead of proceeding onward to "Haftarah" (text, pp. 15–22), you may wish to skip to the chapter on Minhag. Note especially the "Have You Heard?" distinguishing Halachah from Mitzvah and Minhag (p. 66). In introducing "B.C.E." and "C.E.," you may wish to refer to the time line on p. 19.

Answers to "Review It" Questions: p. 13: (1) fast, wash for health purposes but not for pleasure, leave off perfumes and body oils, don't wear leather shoes; p. 14: (1) the Torah is not in heaven but was given to humanity at Mount Sinai.

Answers to Student Activity Book Questions: p. 11: (1) guide, (2) interpret, (3) interpreters, (4) majority, (5) change; p. 13: (1) Jewish law or "the path to walk upon."

CHAPTER THREE

HAFTARAH

Objectives

1. To introduce Haftarah as the reading from the Prophets that comes at the conclusion of the Torah ceremony.

2. To show how the Haftarah amplifies or modifies the Torah reading.

3. To offer two possible explanations for the origin of the practice of reading the Haftarah.

Background

The Haftarah, the passage from one of the books of the Nevi'im that follows the Torah reading on Shabbat and holidays, is the bridge that links the Torah of Moses with the teachings of the Prophets. Although the prophetic literature is the source of the Haftarah readings, the literature of the Prophets is not synonymous with Haftarah. Only certain passages from the Nevi'im make up the Haftarot.

The chapter offers two explanations for the origin of the practice of Haftarah; each hinges on the question of whether, like the Torah, the words of the Prophets are sacred literature. In the development of the Jewish worship service, retention of the readings from the Prophets long after the threat from the Samaritans and Antiochus had faded was not just a matter of preference but involved the belief that the Haftarah *had* to be read along with the Torah. This implied a recognition that the Torah portion was somehow incomplete without its complementary Haftarah.

If we study carefully the relationship between Haftarah and Torah portion, we can see that that the Prophets put a different emphasis on Jewish practice than does the Torah. The text conveys this lesson in its discussion of the Book of Jonah (pp. 17–19), which softens the notion of God as a stern judge by portraying Him as ever merciful to all peoples. A classic example of how the Haftarah modifies the emphasis of the Torah reading involves the portion Tzav and its corresponding Haftarah from Jeremiah. Parashat Tzav (Leviticus 6:1–7:38) deals in elaborate detail with sacrificial ritual, spelling out precisely how the burnt offering, meal offering, sin offering, guilt offering, and sacrifice of well-being are to be made. The opening lines of the Haftarah from Jeremiah (7:21–8:3; 9:22–23) are startlingly blunt in casting aside ritual where righteousness is absent:

Thus said the Lord of Hosts, the God of Israel: Add your burnt offerings to your other sacrifices and eat the meat!

For when I freed your fathers from the land of Egypt, I did not speak with them or command them concerning burnt offerings or sacrifice.

But this is what I commanded them: Do My bidding, that I may be your God and you may be My people; walk only in the way that I enjoin upon you, that it may go well with you. (Jeremiah 7:21–23)

Doubtless many worshipers in Diaspora after the Second Temple was destroyed took comfort in Jeremiah's message that God's will could still be carried out even though the sacrificial rituals were no longer being conducted.

Words to the Wise

Key terms:

Antiochus

Babylonia

*Haftarah (הַפְטָרָה)

*Nevi'im

Nineveh, Ninevites

Samaria, Samaritans

Other terms:

begrudge

exile

emphasis

repent

Delving into the Chapter

Go over the definition of "Haftarah" with the class (text, p. 15), emphasizing that the Haftarah may explain, interpret, broaden, or even contradict the meaning of the Torah portion. The Haftarah Noah (Isaiah 54:1–55:5, esp. 54:7–8) offers an interpretation of the Torah portion that includes the story of Noah and the flood (Genesis 6:9–9:29); the Jonah Haftarah (text, pp. 18–19) broadens the Yom Kippur theme of repentance and forgiveness to include all people, not only Jews. For an example of a Haftarah that apparently argues with the Torah portion, see the discussion of Haftarat Tzav above.

A discussion of Jonah's behavior toward non-Jews might provoke some interesting responses. Contrast Jonah's willingness to allow the destruction of the Ninevites with the way he is treated by the sailors on the ship. These sailors do not want any harm to befall Jonah even after they become convinced that his attempt to flee God is the cause of the storm that endangers all their lives. You may also want to contrast Jonah's anger at the withering of the vine (which had sheltered him from the heat of the sun) with his callousness toward the lives of 120,000 Ninevites. What is the Haftarah saying about the relation between concern for our own comfort—or, appropriately for Yom Kippur, our own afflictions—and concern for the needs of others? "Jonah's Journey" (Student Activity Book, p. 15), which offers an intensive verbal and pictorial review of the Jonah story, would be appropriate at this point.

Ask your students: How does Haftarah show that Judaism is always growing? The answer, which hinges on the way the Prophets broadened and reinterpreted the message of Torah, can be related back to the chapter on Halachah, which offers another means of reinterpreting Torah. The constant reexamining of Torah makes Judaism a dynamic religion. The reading of Haftarah is part of the process of growth and change.

In conjunction with the time line (text, p. 19), discuss the two explanations for the origin of the practice of reading the Haftarah. Point out where Antiochus appears on the time line. Ask students where they would locate the first Samaritans; the text (p. 20) gives a figure of "nearly 28 centuries," which would date the Samaritans to the period between Moses and the destruction of the First Temple. If you've recently read the Halachah chapter, ask students if they recall the story of Moses and Akiba (text, p. 11). Note that the time lapse between Moses and Akiba is *less* than the span between Akiba and our own day.

Up for Discussion

1. Through the discussion of Aggadah and Halachah, Torah and Haftarah, the idea of unity in diversity should already be evolving in your classroom. But what does the idea of unity in diversity mean? Have students name some different things that when put together form a whole, a unity, a completeness. An example might be as simple as a salad: you might want to try a co-op salad, with each student bringing a piece of fruit or a vegetable to class—you furnish the bowl and the utensils! Having the class work on a jigsaw puzzle might convey the same idea. Another example of unity emerging from diversity is an automobile on an assembly line. Perhaps one of your scholars will offer as an example a person's life. If not, you can introduce the idea that we are all formed of many "pieces"—our unique experiences, lessons we learn, parental and family influences, etc. We become more complete as we add to and develop ourselves.

2. The two suggested explanations for the Haftarah reading are examples of practices that have become traditions. Can students cite any examples from their own lives of practices that have become family or personal traditions? Maybe one year someone got tickets for the whole family to go to a baseball game, and everyone enjoyed the day so much that a family baseball outing has become an annual tradition. Family picnics, cookouts, and barbecues offer rich examples of such traditions: the same favorite stories are told at family get-togethers year after year, the same special dishes are made, and the cook may even wear the same favorite hat or apron. The material is there, but you, the teacher, have to find the right prods to bring it out.

Write On!

1. Present students with appropriate excerpts from the Torah portion and Haftarah read in synagogue that week. Have each student write a paragraph explaining how that week's Haftarah amplifies the Torah. Students can then read their interpretations to the rabbi for comment.

2. Antiochus has been defeated, and the Temple restored. Have students write, individually or collectively, a playlet in which a group of scholars debate whether Haftarah readings should continue. What are the arguments for and against?

3. Assign each student to write a brief story, true or fictional, in which someone does something wrong but avoids a punishment by apologizing sincerely.

4. Ask each student to write three brief paragraphs describing the three figures (e.g., parent, other relative, teacher, rabbi, fictional character, celebrity) who have contributed most to his/her becoming a "whole" person. How did each figure help the student become more "complete"?

And Finally . . .

Student Activity Book pp. 14, 16, and 17 ("Take Five") can be used for drill and review.

NOTE: You may proceed onward to the Ḥumash chapter (text, pp. 23–30). The Nevi'im chapter (pp. 75–82) might also be an effective followup.

Answers to "Review It" Questions: p. 19: (1) the ways of the non-Jewish peoples of Egypt and Canaan; (2) c, d.

Answers to Student Activity Book Questions: p. 14: (1) b, (2) c, (3) a, (4) b, (5) a; p. 15: Israel, great fish, Nineveh, Tigris; p. 17: (1) conclusion; (2) Nevi'im; (3) explain or amplify the Torah reading, emphasize that the prophets spoke the word of God; (4) Samaritans.

CHAPTER FOUR

ḤUMASH

Objectives

1. To introduce the Ḥumash as the Five Books of Moses.

2. To describe the structure of the Ḥumash and the literary techniques it embodies.

3. To show that the Ḥumash offers a psychologically realistic portrayal of our ancestors, including their human failings and ambitions.

Background

Even students who have trouble grasping the difference between Aggadah and Halachah or between Mitzvah and Minhag should have little difficulty understanding the meaning and derivation of the term "Ḥumash."

Until the twentieth century, every Jew knew what the Ḥumash was, and everyone studied "Ḥumash with Rashi" (see the Rashi chapter, pp. 109–14). The term is less commonly used today, but it remains basic to the vocabulary of Jewish experience, especially as distinguished from Sefer Torah (the Torah scroll) and Tanach (the whole of the Hebrew Bible). Every Sefer Torah contains the Ḥumash, inscribed in the ritually correct manner, but the text of the Ḥumash can appear in many forms, most commonly as the first five books of a bound Bible, or as the printed Hebrew-English text followed by the congregation during the reading of the weekly Torah portion. The whole of the Ḥumash is found in every Hebrew Bible, but many Biblical books and characters are not found in the Ḥumash.

"Ḥumash" comes from the root meaning "five" (or a fifth), so it means something like "five times" or "fiver"; the link, of course, is to the Five Books of Moses. Given the simplicity of this connection, the chapter focuses not on the concept of Ḥumash but on the many wonderful stories the Ḥumash contains. Remember that the text deals mostly with the narratives of the Ḥumash, and not the legal portions or the poetic material. You should bring to the classroom your own knowledge and love of the Ḥumash, and freely share them with your students. Make sure the class knows how many favorite stories and characters are found in the Ḥumash: the Creation, Noah and the flood, Abraham and Sarah, Joseph, the great liberation epic of Exodus, and the original laws of the Hebrew people, including the Ten Commandments, or Aseret HaDibrot (text, pp. 95–102).

Feel free to deal with the excitement of personalities, the great story cycles, and the familiar tales of our patriarchs and matriarchs. Do not neglect, however, the great and exalting message to be found in the very shape of the Ḥumash. The first eleven chapters of the Humash—of the entire Bible, for that matter—deal with the history (mythically told) of the universe. Only after the origins of time, space, the celestial bodies, plant and animal life, humanity and human passions, language, and the cycles of work and rest and of creation and destruction have been accounted for does the Ḥumash zero in on the origins of the Hebrew people. This kind of "midrashic fact" conveys the idea that Jewish tradition, even when telling its own developmental history, views itself only in the context of the world as a whole.

Words to the Wise

If you choose to emphasize recognition of the English and Hebrew names of the Five Books of Moses, make sure students understand the difference between the meaning of the title of the book in English (column two of the table on p. 26 of the text) and the literal meaning of the Hebrew title (column four). You can use Duplicating Master #2 for drill or diagnostic purposes.

Key terms:

Five Books of Moses

*Ḥumash (חוּמָשׁ)

*Ketuvim

*Nevi'im

Pentateuch

Other terms:

birthright

fugitive

kinsmen

personalities

Promised Land

significant

Books of the Ḥumash (in sequence):

Genesis	בְּרֵאשִׁית
Exodus	שְׁמוֹת
Leviticus	וַיִּקְרָא
Numbers	בְּמִדְבַּר
Deuteronomy	דְּבָרִים

Delving into the Chapter

Introduce the definition on p. 23 of the text, making sure that students grasp the link between Ḥumash, five, the Five Books of Moses, and the Greek root of Pentateuch, which also means "five" (compare, for example, pentangle and pentagon). Go over the chart on p. 26 of the text and then have students do p. 18 of the Student Activity Book.

Several stories in this chapter lend themselves to dramatization. A group of students can be asked to dramatize the story of how Rebecca and Jacob fooled Isaac into giving Jacob his blessing; alternatively, three smaller groups of students can write scripts for the three "well stories" (Isaac and Rebecca, Jacob and Rachel, Moses and

Zipporah) and present them to the class. After the presentations, discuss with the class the similarities and differences the three stories show.

If your class is not familiar with the story of Cain and Abel, retell or read it. Ask your students to compare it with the story of Esau and Jacob.

- What common elements do these stories have?
- How realistically does the Humash portray the rivalry between brothers?

Expand the second "Review It" question on p. 28 of the text and/or the "Trickery" exercise on p. 19 of the Student Activity Book:

- Why does the Humash insist on showing us the weak points of our ancestors as well as the strong points?
- What lessons can we draw from what happens to people in the Bible as a result of their character flaws?
- How can studying the good and bad points of our ancestors help us evaluate our own strengths and weaknesses?
- What is a hero? Does the Humash have heroes and heroines? How do the human heroes and heroines of the Humash differ from such "superheroes" as Superman and Wonder Woman? Is God the "superhero" of the Bible?

Up for Discussion

1. This chapter retells three stories from Humash for which a well provides the setting. Ask students why they think the well played such an important role in Biblical times. (Besides the obvious need for water, the well was a communications center, a place to exchange information and ideas.) If the Humash were being written today, where might Jacob and Rachel be likely to meet? What are today's most common meeting places for young people? Students might want to ask their parents where they first met and report to the class on the findings.

2. Ask the class if anyone can guess why so many words having to do with the Bible—including the word "Bible" itself—come from Greek. Explain the Greek domination of Near Eastern land and culture that followed the conquests of Alexander the Great (d. 323 B.C.E.). You can find a discussion of this period in any full-length Jewish history; see, for example, Abba Eban's *Heritage: Civilization and the Jews*, pp. 73–77. Can students identify any examples of Greek influence in the world today? (Architecture, the Olympic games, the Hippocratic Oath taken by physicians, many words with Greek roots, etc.)

Write On!

1. Bible stories tell us how people lived in early days. After going over the chapter with your students, have them write a paragraph explaining some of the customs, beliefs, and conditions that were characteristic of Bible times. Examples might include the birthright, kinds of food, and marriage customs. Students should be encouraged to include illustrations with their written descriptions.

2. The Ḥumash describes Isaac's marriage as arranged by a matchmaker and the fathers of Leah, Rachel, and Zipporah "giving" their daughters as wives to Jacob and Moses. Have students compare these customs to our ways of choosing a mate today. What are the advantages and disadvantages of each method? How do the choices open to women today differ from the choices available to them in Bible times? (You might want to play the class a recording of the song "Matchmaker, Matchmaker" from *Fiddler on the Roof* for inspiration!)

3. Isaac and Rebecca each had a favorite son. Have students write a short essay or story showing how they would feel if they were (a) the family favorite or (b) the less favored child.

4. After the class has completed and discussed the exercise on p. 20 of the Student Activity Book, have each student write at least two paragraphs about a role model he or she admires. What special qualities account for the influence of this person?

And Finally...

Use "Take Five" (Student Activity Book, p. 21) for diagnostic purposes or review.

NOTE: The next chapter, Ketuvim (pp. 31–38), discusses another major section of the Bible. You may then elect to follow up with Nevi'im (pp. 75–82) and Tanach (pp. 141–45). Alternatively, the method used in discussing Ḥumash fits well with the Rashi chapter (pp. 109–14). You can point a contrast between Ḥumash as an object of study and as an object of reverence by following up with Sefer Torah (pp. 83–88).

Answers to "Review It" Questions: p. 28: (1) to teach that God created the entire universe; to teach that all people, not merely Jews, are His children; (2) (a) Isaac, (b) Jacob, (c) Esau, (d) Rebecca; p. 30: (1) Rebecca is the stronger of the two personalities; (2) generosity, kindness to animals; (3) his interest in the gifts, the attempt to have Rebecca stay with the family another year before leaving to marry Isaac; (4) saving the girls shows Moses' bravery and kindness; Moses rescued from the Nile (Exodus 2:1–10), waters of Egypt turning to blood (Exodus 7:19–25), the parting of the waters (Exodus 14:21–22), drawing water from a stone (Numbers 20:7–13).

Answers to Student Activity Book Questions: p. 18: Leviticus, Genesis, Exodus, Deuteronomy, Numbers; p. 21: (1) Five Books of Moses, Torah, Pentateuch; (2) d; (3) the story of Creation; see answers to "Review It," p. 28 (1); (4) all take place at well; all lead to marriage; (5) marriages were often arranged by matchmakers; father had right to choose who would become his daughter's husband.

Answers to Duplicating Master #2: Bible, Genesis, בְּרֵאשִׁית, Rebecca, Rachel, Exodus, שְׁמוֹת, Zipporah, Leviticus, חוּמָשׁ, וַיִּקְרָא, בְּמִדְבַּר, Numbers, census, desert, Moses, Deuteronomy, repetition, דְּבָרִים, words, forty.

CHAPTER FIVE

KETUVIM

Objectives

1. To introduce Ketuvim as the third part of the Hebrew Bible, comprising many different types of books.

2. To present the Book of Proverbs as a source of principles of proper behavior, especially concerning parent-child relationships and the importance of learning from others' criticism.

3. To demonstrate the relationship between the five Megillot and the holidays on which they are read.

Background

The superabundance of vocabulary words—books and sections of the Bible, literary forms, holidays—makes this one of the more difficult chapters of the text. Teaching Ketuvim requires time and care. Both this guide and the Student Activity Book offer a variety of activities to allow students to apply their new learning in enjoyable and creative ways.

An entire year could be spent on Ketuvim: a proverb each week, reflecting moral points for the students to accept or question; a psalm each week, to capture every shifting mood; Megillot for each season and many holidays; thoughts from Ecclesiastes that can be applied to well-known stories in the Humash. Of course, you don't have an entire year, but you should attempt to convey to the class the extraordinary variety of experiences and emotions Ketuvim encompasses.

Ketuvim constitutes the third division of the Tanach, Torah (or Humash) and Nevi'im being the first two. The writings within Ketuvim come from separate sources and have their own distinct forms and subjects. They were the last to be canonized—that is, the last to become accepted as sacred literature—and have the least Halachic authority. On the other hand, no other body of Jewish literature offers so many affective opportunities, ranging from the drama of Ruth and the Song of Songs to the historical specificity of Lamentations, the challenging perplexities of Job, the changing emotions of the Psalms, and the moral argument of Proverbs and Ecclesiastes.

Words to the Wise

Key words:

*Ketuvim (כְּתוּבִים)

*Megillah (מְגִלָּה), Megillot (מְגִלּוֹת)

*Nevi'im (נְבִיאִים)

*Tanach (תַּנַ"ךְ)

*Torah (תּוֹרָה)

Books of the Ketuvim (in order):

Psalms	תְּהִלִּים
Proverbs	מִשְׁלֵי
Job	אִיּוֹב
Song of Songs	שִׁיר הַשִּׁירִים
Ruth	רוּת
Lamentations	אֵיכָה
Ecclesiastes	קֹהֶלֶת
Esther	אֶסְתֵּר
Daniel	דָּנִיאֵל
Ezra	עֶזְרָא
Nehemiah	נְחֶמְיָה
I Chronicles	דִּבְרֵי הַיָּמִים א
II Chronicles	דִּבְרֵי הַיָּמִים ב

Holidays mentioned:

Pesaḥ

Purim

Shavuot

Sukkot

Tisha b'Av

Other terms:

Babylonian exile

criticism

devour

elegy

flattery

maxims

meditations

Moabite

offense

Delving into the Chapter

Read and discuss together the introductory material on pp. 31–33 of the chapter; this will give students a good idea of the meaning of Ketuvim and what it contains. Spend some time going over the chart so that students can become familiar with the English and Hebrew titles and the content summaries. For reinforcement you can use the "Ketuvim Crossword" (Duplicating Master #3); alternatively, play "Hangman" with some of the chart words, hold a spelling and defining bee, or have students match up the English and Hebrew titles (which you have written on cards in advance) or each book and its appropriate theme or season.

As an introduction to the Book of Proverbs, give each student a strip of paper with a proverb written on it. Some examples might be:

- A penny saved is a penny earned.
- God helps those who help themselves.
- Little strokes fell great oaks.

- Different strokes for different folks.
- Pride goes before a fall.
- Hope deferred makes the heart sick.
- A soft answer turns away wrath.
- A bird in the hand is worth two in the bush.
- Make hay while the sun shines.
- An ounce of prevention is worth a pound of cure.
- A rolling stone gathers no moss.
- Rome was not built in a day.
- Look before you leap.
- Out of the frying pan into the fire.
- If you can't stand the heat, get out of the kitchen.
- Sticks and stones may break my bones, but names can never hurt me.
- Spare the rod and spoil the child.
- One good turn deserves another.
- The buck stops here.
- It's better to live one day as a lion than a hundred years as a sheep.
- Better red than dead. (Or: Better dead than red.)
- It's not over 'til it's over.
- There's many a slip 'twixt the cup and the lip.
- Many hands make light work.
- The only thing we have to fear is fear itself.
- It's better to have loved and lost than never loved at all.
- It's not whether you win or lose; it's how you play the game.
- Winning isn't everything; it's the only thing.

Have each student read his/her proverb aloud and attempt to explain its meaning. Furnish the explanation if the class can't. Ask your students if they can supply an example of a case in which the proverb might be *true*; next, ask for an example of a case in which that same proverb would be *false*. Note that in some cases proverbs contradict each other. The last two proverbs on the list offer a good example of this.

Today's proverbs come from many sources: the Bible, the writings of Benjamin Franklin and other authors, statements of public figures, folk wisdom, even popular songs. Explain that proverbs urge people to develop such virtues as responsibility, honesty, loyalty, and faithfulness. A proverb usually states a truth or a piece of advice simply and in a way that is easy to memorize.

Share with your students the insight that the Book of Proverbs in Ketuvim is a book of advice, much of it given specifically by an older man to a younger one. Then go over the section on pp. 33–35 of the text. How kindly do your students take to the urgings of the chapter?

The second "Review It" question on p. 35 of the text offers students an opportunity to write their own proverbs.

Up for Discussion

1. Criticism may wear two faces—negative or positive. Can your students define the difference between the two? Which is easier to take? For any or all of the following examples, ask students to supply an example of negative or positive criticism:

- You were on the family phone for a whole hour. Your family reacts.
- The family is going out to a fancy restaurant and you put on a beat-up pair of jeans. Your parents react.
- You were out sick yesterday and came to class unprepared. Your teacher reacts.
- Your best friend offered to paint your portrait and it came out looking really ugly. You react.

After the discussion, have the class complete the self-evaluation exercise on p. 23 of the Student Activity Book. How well did your students rate?

2. In the autumn we celebrate two harvest holidays—can students name them? (Sukkot and Thanksgiving.) Have students compare and contrast the two holidays in terms of foods, customs, and origin. Can the class think of any possible historical connection between the two?

Write On!

1. Read to the class or write on the chalkboard the famous lines from Ecclesiastes 3:1–8. For additional inspiration, play the Byrds' folk-rock setting of the same verses ("Turn, Turn, Turn"). Have students draw a composite "portrait of life" showing some of the many activities the verses describe.

2. Guide the students through the "Poetry Pages" (Student Activity Book, pp. 24–25). Have students copy their cinquains neatly onto a separate sheet of paper and pass them up to you. Then you can read some of the best to the class and/or post them on the bulletin board.

And Finally . . .

Use the "Take Five" (Student Activity Book, p. 26) for reinforcement or evaluation.

NOTE: The next chapter, Leshon HaKodesh (text, pp. 39–44), offers further opportunities for Hebrew practice. Alternatively, you may wish to proceed to Nevi'im (pp. 75–82) and/or Tanach (pp. 141–45).

Answers to "Review It" Questions: p. 38: (1) Lamentations, Ecclesiastes; (2) Purim is a popular holiday, the celebration of which centers around the reading of Megillat Esther in the synagogue.

Answers to Student Activity Book Questions: p. 22: all are אֱמֶת except (2) God, (3) Proverbs, (5) different holidays, (6) Purim, (9) Solomon, (10) David; p. 26: (1) writings; (2) scroll; (3) (a) Esther, (b) Ruth, (c) Ecclesiastes, (d) Song of Songs; (5) (a) Psalms, (b) Proverbs, (c) Job, (d) Song of Songs, (e) Esther, (f) Lamentations, (g) Ecclesiastes, (h) Ruth.

CHAPTER SIX

LESHON HAKODESH

Objectives

1. To introduce the traditional concept of Hebrew as Leshon HaKodesh, the "holy language," and to discuss the meanings we have come to attach to that idea.

2. To show the ways Jews have demonstrated their love for and fascination with Leshon HaKodesh.

3. To demonstrate the achievement of Eliezer ben Yehuda in turning Leshon HaKodesh into a spoken language.

Background

At this point in history, "Leshon HaKodesh" as a synonym for Hebrew has taken on a meaning quite independent of the idea of holiness from which the term derives. We call Hebrew "Leshon HaKodesh" in an affectionate way that emphasizes the connection between the "holy language" and the "Holy Land," where Hebrew is spoken today. Ironically, the Holy Land is now part of a secular state, and the Hebrew language has developed much of its power under the impact of the everyday secular needs of the Israelis who live there. This relation between the sacred and the secular is taken up later, under the heading "Up for Discussion."

The chapter jumps from the Biblical epoch to the Talmudic period, to Rashi, and to the relatively recent accomplishments of Eliezer ben Yehuda. In a way this is misleading, for between the eras of Rashi and Ben Yehuda, Hebrew was not so ossified as the chapter seems to imply. In the Spain of HaLevi, the Egypt of Maimonides, and the Safed of Luria—to give only three well-known examples—Hebrew developed in much the same way as did Halachah, respecting the past but adapting to the needs of new times and places. Doubtless the most vivid example of such adaptation occurs in the modern period, with all its technological richness and intercultural contact; nor should we minimize Ben Yehuda's remarkable achievement. But in one way or another, it has always been Hebrew's task to adapt, to remain a living language.

The number games and mnemonics reflect a special attitude about Hebrew. But the truth is that every culture has viewed its language as something special: just ask anyone who regularly plays Scrabble or Boggle, makes a hobby of crossword puzzles, anagrams, or double-crostics, or follows avidly the prescriptive linguistics of Edwin Newman, William Safire, and other popular wordsmiths. For centuries, if a household had just one book, that book was the Bible. Today, throughout the English-speaking world, is there a home or office library without a dictionary of the English language?

Words to the Wise

Key terms:

*Haggadah

Ḥumash

*Leshon HaKodesh (לְשׁוֹן הַקֹּדֶשׁ)

plagues

*Talmud

Other terms:

conversational

inappropriate

mnemonic device

Delving into the Chapter

Read and discuss the definition of Leshon HaKodesh on p. 39 of the text. Make sure students understand what a mnemonic device is (text, pp. 41–42) and what it's used for. Have students make up mnemonic devices in English for the days of the week (starting with Sunday), the months of the year (starting with January), the months of the Hebrew calendar (Tishri, Heshvan, Kislev, Tevet, Shevat, Adar, Nisan, Iyar, Sivan, Tammuz, Av, Elul), or any other topic you can devise (e.g., American cities with more than 1 million people, ingredients in a favorite recipe, nations of the Middle East). Continue with p. 27 of the Student Activity Book.

Have your students turn to the list of Hebrew number values on p. x of the text. Make sure the class understands that each Hebrew letter has a particular number value. Test your students' understanding by selecting specific letters and calling on individual students to supply the number value for each letter you name. Then write any or all of the following Hebrew words and phrases on the chalkboard and have your students calculate the value:

אֶרֶץ יִשְׂרָאֵל   לְשׁוֹן הַקֹּדֶשׁ

יַיִן   שַׁבָּת שָׁלוֹם

סוֹד   הֲלָכָה

After your students have calculated the values for יַיִן and סוֹד, refer them to the first "Review It" question on p. 43 of the text. For further exercises in Hebrew-English Gematria, use Duplicating Master #4, which is recommended as homework.

Go over with the class the accomplishments of Ben Yehuda. Supplement the discussion with pp. 28–30 of the Student Activity Book.

If the class didn't attempt the patchwork tapestry described in connection with the introductory chapter, now would be a good time to try it. See pp. xvii of this Teacher's Guide.

Up for Discussion

1. Inventing new words goes on all the time in almost every language. Have students make up names for each of the following inventions (or other verbal inventions of your own devising):

- A machine that picks potatoes, peels them, and makes crisp latkes.
- A machine that plucks chicken feathers, cooks the fowl, and makes chicken soup for Shabbat.
- A gadget that turns stale bagels into fashionable jewelry and accessories.
- A pencil that will automatically (and accurately!) write in English or Hebrew depending on which setting is used.

After the names are chosen, you can have your students illustrate one or more of these inventions. Encourage students to make up, name, and illustrate their own inventions.

2. What is a "holy language"? How can a language deal with the daily necessities of life—fixing breakfast, making your bed, taking out the garbage, going to the bathroom—yet still be considered holy? In going over the second "Review It" question on p. 44 of the text, you may wish to consider the following quotation from Nathan Ausubel (*The Book of Jewish Knowledge*, p. 199):

> Jews considered that if [Hebrew] had survived the vicissitudes and determined efforts made for its suppression by the enemies of Israel over several thousand years, beginning with Antiochus Epiphanes, then it was, clearly, not merely a "language" but a "miracle of God." Moreover, it held for them a special meaning in terms of religious nationalism. It constituted a bond linking the past with the present and the present with a glorified promised future that the devout believed would be without end. The Hebrew language thus formed an integral, and even mystical, part of the grand Messianic design of the Hebrew people.

One idea you might develop with students is that the idea of holiness need not be opposed to the everyday. If by holiness we mean a special bond with God and with the Jewish past and the Jewish future, then holiness does not exclude the everyday but instead infuses even the most mundane tasks with special meaning.

Write On!

1. Assign written and/or oral reports on any of the following topics:

(a) The life of Ben Yehuda
(b) How the Hebrew alphabet developed
(c) Languages spoken in Israel today

2. Have students write a brief story describing a visit to a shopping mall or supermarket—how they got there, the items they saw, what they bought, how they (or their parents) paid for their purchases. Ask students to underline each word they think represents an idea or invention introduced since 1881 (when Ben Yehuda first came to Eretz Yisrael).

3. Many words have come into English as borrowings from other languages: taco, mayonnaise, sauerkraut, sushi, and bagel are obvious examples (surely the class can supply more). But suppose English couldn't expand by "loan" words and each new idea had to be described by combining other words from the language's limited word stock.

Write the following list of words on the chalkboard or distribute it to the students on a sheet of paper:

see	near	over	light	machine
touch	far	across	big	human
taste	round	land	funny	grow
smell	picture	water	long	tall
feel	sound	sky	hot	food
hear	under	fast	place	not

Now ask students, *using only the words above*, to write down new names for the following inventions:

refrigerator (example: *not-hot-place-food*)

telephone	computer	spacecraft
airplane	pizza	submarine
microwave oven	television	robot

Have students share their new words with the rest of the class.

You should point out that this is the way many new words in Hebrew were actually constructed. For example, the modern Hebrew word for bulldozer, דְחְפוֹר, represents a combination of the Hebrew words for "push" (דְחַף) and "dig" (חָפַר). Of course, this is not the only way that new words in Hebrew are formed. Unlike English, Hebrew is a highly infixed language—that is, the whole vocabulary grows out of root meanings through the addition of inflectional elements. For example, the Hebrew words סֵפֶר, סִפּוּר, and סִפֵּר all share the same root, while their English equivalents—*book, story,* and *to tell*—do not.

And Finally . . .

Assign "Take Five" (Student Activity Book, p. 31) for practice and review.

NOTE: On the subject of Gematria and other forms of word play, refer to the Introduction (text, pp. 1–2) and "Tanach" (pp. 141–45).

Answers to "Review It" Questions: p. 43: (1) 70; too much wine can lead the drinker to give away secrets; p. 44; (1) many new developments had taken place in science, politics, and literature that Hebrew did not yet have words to describe.

Answers to Student Activity Book Questions: p. 27: Ḥumash, Ketuvim, Nevi'im; p. 31: (1) the holy language; (2) Eliezer ben Yehuda; (3) some Jews thought Hebrew was so holy it shouldn't be used for everyday conversation; others thought Hebrew lacked sufficient vocabulary to deal with modern developments; (4) Yiddish, Russian, English, Arabic, German, etc. **Something Special:** דְּצַךְ עֲדַ"שׁ בְּאַחַ"ב; (1) blood, (2) frogs, (3) lice, (4) flies, (5) cattle disease, (6) boils, (7) hail, (8) locusts, (9) darkness, (10) death of the firstborn; (1) דָם, (2) צְפַרְדֵּעַ (3) כִּנִּים (4) עָרֹב (5) דֶּבֶר (6) שְׁחִין (7) בָּרָד (8) אַרְבֶּה, (9) חֹשֶׁךְ, (10) מַכַּת בְּכוֹרוֹת.

Answers to Duplicating Master #4: Genesis 7:8; Exodus 8:8; Leviticus 1:2; Numbers 9:2; Deuteronomy 1:10.

CHAPTER SEVEN
MIDRASH

Objectives

1. To introduce Midrash as a type of Jewish literature devoted to Bible interpretation.

2. To discuss some of the Midrashim in the Passover Haggadah.

3. To show how the Midrash uses the Bible to illustrate the Mitzvot.

Background

What's the difference between Midrash and Aggadah? Earlier we described Aggadah as a way of presenting great moral and ethical values through stories, parables, and maxims. Aggadah embraces many forms, and many genres may contain Aggadic material. Midrash, on the other hand, is a specific literary genre: a type of Biblical commentary that may include exegesis, sermons, Aggadah, and Halachah. The special way the Bible puts words together, apparent contradictions in a text, the order in which stories are told—all these become grist for the Midrashic mill.

Examples of Midrashim abound. The Leshon HaKodesh chapter (text, p. 41) opens with a Midrash: the interpretation of why the Torah begins with bet rather than alef. The Midrash chapter offers several different Midrashim all based on the same line of the Passover Haggadah, each looking at the same words from a different point of view. The Midrash is the source for some of our best-known stories: Abraham smashing his father's idols, the waters of the Red Sea not parting until the first Israelite took the first fateful step. These stories are so familiar we tend to forget that they come from the Midrash and not from the Bible itself.

Another characteristic Midrash grows out of the Book of Jonah. Why does the prophet refuse to answer God's call? The Midrash answers this question by asserting that Jonah refused the challenge because he didn't want to make Israel look bad. (Since Nineveh was going to repent, God would be reminded of Israel's failure to do so, and thus judge Israel more harshly.) This Midrashic justification of the prophet is also a wonderful way to make a statement about our duty to our children, for the Midrash goes on to say that the prophets were more attentive to the children (Israel) than to the parent (God).

The chapter sometimes uses the term Midrash (plural: Midrashim) to refer to a specific interpretation; at other times, *the* Midrash refers to a genre or body of work. Thus, the Passover Haggadah is said to be both a Midrash and to contain many Midrashim. You should also be aware that the term "Midrash" is today used in a looser sense, as any kind of commentary or interpretation, especially one involving a Biblical theme. The way in which a painter elaborates on a Biblical tale is sometimes called midrashic, as is the ability of a musical score to "comment" on a literary text.

Words to the Wise

Key Terms:

hospitable, hospitality

*Humash

idol

interpretation

*Midrash (מִדְרָשׁ)

*Tanach

Passover terms:

*Haggadah (הַגָּדָה), Haggadot (הַגָּדוֹת)

hametz

maror

matzah

seder

Delving into the Chapter

The elements of Midrash can be shown dynamically in the introductory story of Abraham, Terah, and the idols.

- Does this story appear in the Bible? The answer is no. But the two principal characters in the story, Abraham and Terah, do appear in the Humash.
- What did people believe before Abraham's time? What kind of gods did they pray to?
- What did Abraham believe? How did his beliefs about God differ from those of people before him?
- Did Terah believe in idols? If he didn't, why did he make them?
- Which of the Ten Commandments does this Midrash illustrate? (If students don't know, have them turn to p. 102 of the text.)

The section on the Passover Haggadah (text, pp. 48–50) can be treated in several ways. You can explore the major themes of the Haggadah—the imperative of freedom, the importance of teaching the Passover story to our children—by bringing into the classroom several beautifully illustrated Haggadot from your synagogue library. Students can also be urged to bring in the Haggadot their families use. Notice how different artists portray the four sons, and point out to your students that, in a way, each artist is making a Midrash on the Passover story. Follow up with pp. 32–33 of the Student Activity Book.

You may want to pay particular attention to the use of the word "son" in the story of the four sons. Does this mean that daughters shouldn't be taught about Pesah? Today, increasingly, we speak of "children" rather than "sons" and of "humanity" rather than "man" or "mankind." These broader meanings may well have been present in the text from the beginning, but our increased commitment to inclusive language shows how interpretation of our basic texts continues both to reflect and reshape our changing experiences.

This same process of reflecting and reshaping our experiences underlies the second "Review It" question on p. 50 of the text. Reinterpretation of our experience of oppression has enabled us to sympathize with and support other oppressed peoples. Expand the "Review It" question by pointing to the Jewish involvement in the Russian Revolution of 1917 and in the civil rights movement during the 1960s. To what extent was Jewish involvement in each struggle a source of satisfaction and disappointment? To what extent, if any, do traditional Jewish sympathies for the oppressed affect the treatment of Palestinian Arabs by the State of Israel?

Continue with the Midrashim on hospitality. Try to convey to your students the insight these Midrashim offer into the rabbinic mind. In discussing whether it was proper for Rabban Gamaliel to wait on them, the other rabbis did not just say "OK, he'll serve us this week and we'll serve him next week" or "Let's hire someone to serve us all dinner" or "Let's just go out to eat!" Instead, they looked to scripture to resolve their dilemma. Just as we often look for proper models of behavior in advice columns and etiquette books (Dear Abby, Miss Manners), the rabbis looked for their models of behavior in the Torah and in the oral traditions that had grown up around it. This analogy, though suggestive, is only partly applicable, since etiquette books and advice columns are not divine text. A deeper analogy for the rabbinic use of Torah and tradition might be the way the U.S. Supreme Court looks to the Constitution and to legal precedent in framing its decisions.

You may need to offer your students some guidance on the third "Review It" question (text, p. 52). Consider these examples: (1) A young man at a party is seen drinking several bottles of beer; an hour later, when he offers to take some of his friends for a drive in his car, they politely but firmly say no. (2) You hear on the news that a severe frost has swept Brazil; two weeks later you hear your parents say they've stopped buying coffee because the price in the supermarket is much too high. (3) In London, a young girl looks up at the night sky and sees a fuzzy object in the heavens; seventy-six years later, in Honolulu, an astronomer gazes through a telescope and sees a bright object with a long tail. After solving these puzzles, your students should be able to think of analogous examples from their own lives. This effort to find in events that at first seem unrelated some causal or structural relationship is a very important element in both critical and creative thinking.

Up for Discussion

1. Ask students why they think people worshiped idols in early days. What did these idols represent? (Sun, thunder, oceans, fire, fertility, etc.) Do any religions today represent their gods in the form of statues and sculptures? (Christianity, Buddhism, Hinduism, etc.) In the Midrash about Abraham and the idols, why did the woman offer flour to the idols? It may surprise the class to know that although the ancient Hebrews rejected idol worship, they shared with—or, according to some scholars, adopted from—ancient religions the idea of worshiping God through the sacrifice of grain and meat.

2. Commentaries on the Haggadah show us that a single sentence in the Bible may have many meanings. For each of the following statements of Torah, explore with the class some of the possible meanings.

You shall not murder (Exodus 20:13).

Is it murder to chop down a tree or squish a mosquito? Is it murder to shoot a rabbit in the wild? Suppose you kill someone's pet rabbit—is *that* murder? Is it murder if a soldier kills another soldier in battle? Suppose the soldier shoots a civilian? Is it murder if you kill someone in self-defense? Is abortion murder? What about euthanasia?

You shall have no other gods beside Me (Exodus 20:3).

Does this mean that there are no other gods? Or does it mean that other gods exist but should not be regarded as equal to the God of the Hebrews? Is the commandment telling us that it's acceptable to pray to other gods as long as they're regarded as lesser deities?

I will remember My covenant between Me and you and every living creature among all flesh, so that the waters shall never again become a flood to destroy all flesh (Genesis 9:15).

What does the Bible mean by "every living creature"—are plants, insects, and fish included as well as animals? Does the pledge not to "destroy all flesh" by flood mean that God will never again destroy the world—or only that flooding will not be the chosen means of destruction? What about destruction by fire—or by freezing? If God speaks only to Noah, how can He be said to have a convenant with all living creatures?

Write On!

1. The Midrash says that Moses never did eat dinner the night he entertained Jethro because he was so busy serving his guests. Have each student write a note inviting Moses to Shabbat dinner. Make sure students indicate not only the basic facts (time, date, place) but also the menu and some of the evening's activities. Students may choose to make their invitations in the style of Moses' era or of our own. Encourage the class to make use of basic facts about Moses' life story.

2. Assign "Midrash Detector" (Student Activity Book, p. 34). After students have completed and gone over the exercise, ask them to write a brief paragraph explaining in their own words the difference between Midrash and Aggadah.

3. Have students make up a Midrash based on the Biblical characters Isaac, Rebecca, Jacob, and Esau to illustrate the commandment *Honor your father and mother.*

And Finally . . .

"Take Five" (Student Activity Book, p. 35) provides an opportunity for drill and review.

NOTE: This chapter has many thematic links with the "Aggadah" chapter (text, pp. 3–8) and may directly follow it or precede it. The focus on interpretation of Humash also suggests links with "Humash" (pp. 23–30) and "Rashi" (pp. 109–114).

Answers to "Review It" Questions: p. 50: (1) "You shall tell your son on that day ..."; p. 52: (1) hospitality; (2) Rabban Gamaliel.

Answers to Student Activity Book Questions: p. 34: מִדְרָשׁ should be marked for 1, 2, 4, 7, 9, 10; p. 35: (1) דָּרַשׁ; (2) he made idols; by smashing them; (4) because "this" refers to the matzah and maror on the seder table.

CHAPTER EIGHT

MEZUZAH

Objectives

1. To identify the Mezuzah, describe its design and contents, and indicate how and where it should be installed.

2. To show the value of a Mezuzah as a constant reminder of our relationship with God.

3. To demonstrate how a custom can retain its importance even if the reason for that custom changes.

Background

Since the idea of Mezuzah is not difficult to grasp, you can use this chapter to stress one of the most important themes in the development of Judaism—the coexistence of constancy and change. As should be evident from the photo layout on p. 54 of the text, Mezuzot can be curved or square, twisted or straight, metallic or wooden, elaborate or simple, depending on the spirit of the age and the taste and imagination of the artisan. The parchment, on the other hand, must meet halachic standards, and the Mezuzah must be hung according to prescribed forms and rituals.

Some of the more elegantly decorated Mezuzot shown in the text illustrate a related principle in Jewish life, Hiddur Mitzvah (הדור מִצְוָה), "beautifying the commandment." The making of Mezuzot was one way Jews could exercise their artistic ability. The artistic impulse, creative and individual, was thus made to serve the interests of public piety, which was normative and communal. In practice, the "Hiddur" often overwhelmed the "Mitzvah," but that shouldn't prevent you from exciting your students about the rich artistic possibilities inherent in a strict tradition.

The stories about the miraculous powers of Mezuzot offer yet another variation on the same theme. The commandments of Mezuzah have been fulfilled for two millennia. For much of that period, the Mezuzah was regarded as an amulet, intended to ward off evil. Today we continue to display the Mezuzah, but for very different reasons: to show pride in our Judaism and to identify ourselves to the world as Jewish.

Words to the Wise

Key terms:

*Ḥumash

*Mezuzah (מְזוּזָה), Mezuzot (מְזוּזוֹת)

*Mishnah

*Sefer Torah

*Shaddai (שַׁדַּי)

Shema

Other terms:

doorpost

expulsion

parchment

Parthia, Parthian

token

Delving into the Chapter

You may want to make this a "hands-on" chapter, with each student making a Mezuzah. Ask students to bring to class a matchbox, gift box, juice can, milk carton, or any similar small container. Make sure you have on hand a supply of foil, construction paper, tissue, gift wrap, markers, crayons, and other decorative materials.

The first step is to develop with your students a list of rules for making Mezuzot. Every Mezuzah must:

(1) contain the Shema;

(2) have שׁ or שַׁדַּי visible on the outside;

(3) have holes at top and bottom for attaching to the doorpost;

(4) be fastened to the right-hand side as you enter;

(5) be no more than one-third of the way down from the top of the doorpost.

Write the Shema on the chalkboard, remembering to make the ע and   larger than normal (see p. 88 of the text). Point out to your students that in order for this to be a strictly proper Mezuzah, the Shema would have to be written by a scribe on parchment from a clean animal. Tell them that although they aren't scribes and their paper isn't parchment, they can honor at least part of the commandment by copying the Shema as carefully as possible. Check the "scrolls" before they are rolled up and placed inside the case.

Students can now adorn their cases. Students who are at a loss for decorating ideas should be referred to the photographs in the text. How beautiful can your students make their Mezuzot while still following the rules?

The Student Activity Book (pp. 36–37) offers additional practice in creative Mezuzah-making.

Up for Discussion

1. Go over with the class the story of Onkelos ben Kalonimos. You and your students may well feel a certain skepticism about this story: Does the class really believe that Onkelos could have converted the Roman soldiers to Judaism just by quoting Torah to them? Can people really be so easily swayed as the narrative suggests? Even if you doubt the literal truth of the narrative, you can use the tale to show the way our ancestors employed stories to convey important truths. How did Onkelos' dazzling description of the Mezuzah save him from prison? Can your students think of a time when quick thinking and clever words saved them from trouble? Why didn't Onkelos just give up his adopted religion when the Emperor made Torah study illegal? What does his continued allegiance to Judaism say about Onkelos' character?

2. You may want to treat the Onkelos legend as a tall story or fairy tale. Can students think of any other stories in which a magic potion or lucky charm played an important role? What kinds of things do people today sometimes carry around with them for good luck? (A ḥai around the neck, a rabbit's foot, for Christians a crucifix, etc.)

Write On!

1. Assign special reports, written and/or oral, on Yehudah HaNasi or about the Parthian Empire.

2. Have your students write at least two paragraphs describing something they keep as a good luck charm, e.g., lucky coin, lucky hat, rabbit's foot, teddy bear. Can students cite specific examples of the good luck the lucky charm brought them?

3. Ask students to write a tall story about how a Jewish hero was saved by a Mezuzah. Examples might include a Wild West tale about a Jewish marshal who uses a Mezuzah to defeat a gang of desperados, or a Jewish starfighter who with the help of a Mezuzah conquers an evil empire or rids the universe of malevolent aliens.

And Finally ...

Both the "True or False" exercise and "Take Five" (Student Activity Book, pp. 38–39) provide opportunities for review or diagnostic testing.

NOTE: The next chapter, "Minhag" (text, pp. 61–66), effectively extends the theme of continuity and change in Judaism.

Answers to "Review It" Questions: p. 58: (1) Guardian of the doors of Israel, or שׁוֹמֵר דַּלְתוֹת יִשְׂרָאֵל; p. 60: (1) King Arteban thought an object of value was one that had to be protected (i.e., a gem), while Yehudah HaNasi thought an object of value was one that offers protection (i.e., the teachings of God's Torah); (2) Arteban's gift needed a guard, but Yehudah HaNasi's gift was a guard.

Answers to Student Activity Book Questions: p. 36 (1) Hear, O Israel, the Lord is our God, the Lord is one; p. 38: all are אֱמֶת except (1) may be *or* need not be, (3) doorpost, (5) "Shaddai," (9) studying Torah *or* refusing to obey the Emperor's law, (10) writing on the inside; p. 39: (1) doorpost, (2) all have שׁ or שַׁדַּי visible on the outside, all contain the Shema, etc.; (3) the power to keep Jews safe from harm, (4) he pointed to a Mezuzah and told the soldiers its meaning; the soldiers converted to Judaism; (5) b, d, f, h.

Answers to Duplicating Master #5: GUARDIAN OF THE DOORS OF ISRAEL; שׁוֹמֵר דַּלְתוֹת יִשְׂרָאֵל.

CHAPTER NINE

MINHAG

Objectives

1. To introduce the concept of Minhag as Jewish custom.

2. To distinguish Minhag from Halachah and Mitzvah.

3. To describe various customs for Shabbat and Hanukkah as examples of the way Minhag functions.

Background

The term "Minhag" is not all that familiar to us today, but the idea surely is. Every time we say or hear something like "Uncle Charlie used to do it this way" or "This is how my mother made Shabbos" or "The right way to say this prayer is ..." we may be entering the realm of Minhag, or Jewish custom. Whether we start eating popcorn during the previews or only when the feature begins, how we sit (or stand or lie down) while talking on the telephone, whether we eat the different parts of the main course all at once or one at a time, whether we do the most enjoyable things first or leave the best parts for last—these are matters of personal custom or habit, which might be called Minhag.

Sometimes Minhagim spring up for odd reasons, and then people keep the Minhag but forget how it started. There was once a town in Michigan where all Jewish funerals began at the same time, just before noon. The Minhag originated because the rabbi who presided at funerals had to take a train home by a certain time. After a while, the town got a different rabbi, but the Minhag of having the funeral just before noontime persisted. By then, few people remembered how the Minhag started, and many townsfolk had come to believe that starting a funeral before noon was required by Halachah.

Minhagim, however, are more important than this relatively trivial example implies. Minhagim open a window onto a culture, offering us an opportunity to observe the folkways and life patterns of different groups. They also allow us to invest mandated Halachic practices with some of our most important personal values. Moreover, although the chapter seeks to make a clear distinction between Minhag and Halachah in contemporary Judaism, the importance of Minhag derives in part from the fact that, historically, the distinction has never been nearly so clear-cut. Much of what became Halachah must have started as custom in Hebrew society before the time of Moses. Discussions in the Talmud show tension on the relative claims of custom and law: Halachah was cited both to validate custom and, where the custom was objectionable, to deny it. In such civil matters as the signing of documents and the setting of work hours, the rabbis acknowledged that "custom overrides the law"; this principle was likewise granted in ritual matters, but predominantly in cases where custom made the Halachah more stringent rather than less. If it is true that Halachah is constantly evolving as the conditions of Jewish life change, then Minhag is an instrument in the evolution of Halachah.

We do not have to look hard to find analogous cases in secular life. Often when a statute is widely violated, enforcement becomes slack, and the law is moderated or repealed altogether. Prohibition offers an obvious instance of this principle, and laws banning the use of marijuana, forbidding strikes by public school teachers, and making divorce a difficult and lengthy process offer other examples of cases where public practice has surely diverged from—and sometimes forced changes in—the statutes. Controversies over which films deserve G, PG, PG-13, R, or X ratings show a similar tension between the "Halachah" of Hollywood ratings and the "Minhag" of community standards. What qualifies for a PG-13 today might never have made it into the movie theaters only a generation ago.

Words to the Wise

Key terms:

*Halachah

*Ḥumash

*Mashiaḥ (מָשִׁיחַ), Messiah

*Midrash

*Minhag (מִנְהָג), Minhagim (מִנְהָגִים)

*Mitzvah

Ḥanukkah terms:

Antiochus

dreidel

gelt

latkes

Maccabees

Delving into the Chapter

The Student Activity Book offers exercises based on Minhagim for Shabbat (p. 40) and Ḥanukkah (p. 41). The activity emphasizing the distinction between Mitzvah, Halachah, and Minhag (p. 42) should be offered in conjunction with the discussion of these three concepts (text, pp. 63–64) and the subsequent "Have You Heard?" (text, p. 72). You can reinforce students' awareness of the distinction by asking them to look up the appropriate definitions in the Glossary (text, pp. 146–48) and having them write a brief paragraph comparing Mitzvah, Halachah, and Minhag in their own words.

This chapter provides little opportunity for literary analysis, but it does give you the chance to explore with the class comparative holiday customs (including your own favorites), especially if your study of the chapter falls around Ḥanukkah time. For example, the text mentions latkes and doughnuts, traditional Ḥanukkah foods that are fried in oil. (Make sure the class understands why the use of oil in cooking for this holiday is appropriate.) For Sephardim the typical fried treats for Ḥanukkah are bimuelos or loukomades—deep fried puffs, something like raised doughnuts, dipped in a honey syrup or sprinkled with powdered sugar and/or cinnamon and served warm. Bimuelos at Hanukkah are to the Sephardim what potato latkes are to the Ashkenazim. If you are feeling ambitious, you might want to divide the class into two "communities" and have each group prepare its Hanukkah specialty.

You probably have your own favorite latke recipe, but here's another good one the class might try.

Leah's Latkes

1 small onion, grated

6 potatoes, washed well and grated with skin

2 eggs, beaten

2 tablespoons pancake mix

1 teaspoon salt

Pepper to taste

1/4 teaspoon baking powder

Cooking oil for frying

First grate the onion, then grate the potatoes—a food processor may also be used. Combine all the ingredients except the oil in a large mixing bowl. (A pinch of baking soda will help keep the potatoes from turning brown.) Heat oil 1/4 inch deep in a frying pan. Drop the batter 1 tablespoon at a time into the hot fat. Turn the latkes only once, so they don't get soggy; latkes are done when they're dark and crisp around the edges. Serve with sour cream and/or apple sauce. Yield: 24–30 latkes.

The recipe for bimuelos comes from the Greek island of Rhodes. Although the puffs are best when made fresh and served immediately, they can be fried ahead of time and dipped in the hot syrup just before serving.

Bimuelos (Loukomades)

1 1/3 cup warm water

2 cakes yeast (room temperature)

1 egg

1/2 teaspoon salt

1 tablespoon cooking oil

3 cups flour, unsifted

Cinnamon for sprinkling

Oil for deep frying

Syrup

1 24-oz. jar honey

1/4 cup water

Combine honey and water for syrup; bring to a boil, then keep warm. Dissolve yeast in $\frac{1}{2}$ cup of warm water. Add beaten egg, salt, and cooking oil to mixture. Add flour all at once and stir, adding remaining water gradually. Allow the dough at least 1 hour to rise. (This is a good time to have the class play dreidel.) Heat cooking oil to about 375°F. After dipping a tablespoon in the hot oil, drop the batter one spoonful at a time into the hot fat. Bimuelos puff up and should be turned until evenly golden. Drain on paper towels. Dip bimuelos in warm syrup and sprinkle generously with cinnamon. Yield: about 4 dozen.

Make sure the class understands that the difference between Sephardic and Ashkenazic cooking reflects the difference between the foods grown and eaten in Germany and Eastern Europe and those popular along the Mediterranean and in the Middle East. Use a map to make the geographical distinctions clear.

Up for Discussion

1. Let's return to the idea of personal Minhagim. Ask students what customs their families follow when celebrating a birthday. Does the family eat foods that are the special favorites of the honored person? Are there any special rituals that go with birthday celebrations? Do your students celebrate the birthdays of their pets or—stretching things a bit—of favorite dolls or stuffed animals? (One family dog, who loved cherry pie, was allowed once a year, on her birthday, to sit on a chair and eat a piece of her favorite dessert from the dinner table with the rest of the family!)

2. How can special customs unite a family? How do customs make a family unique? Some families hold annual reunions at which the same special foods are prepared and the same stories told and retold. Others hold a family picnic, make an annual trip to a ballgame, or circulate a newsy round-robin letter at the end of each year. Ask students to identify customs that are unique to their own (extended) family. Can they trace the origins of some of their family customs?

Communal Minhagim, which emerge out of the combined force of personal and family preferences, create the pressure that often leads to changes in Halachah. How do customs make a people or community unique? How do customs hold a people or group together? How can this feeling of togetherness help during hard times or periods of oppression?

3. Invite your own rabbi or one from a different congregation to talk with the class about the ways Ashkenazic and Sephardic holiday and Shabbat Minhagim differ.

Write On!

1. Special reports (written and/or oral):
Origins of the Ashkenazim and Sephardim
What is Yiddish?
Ḥanukkah customs around the world

2. Have students write letters to Judah Maccabee inviting him to a Ḥanukkah party. The letter should explain to Judah how the foods and activities planned for the party reflect the holiday's history and meaning. It should also tell Judah about any Ḥanukkah Minhagim adopted since his time.

3. On pieces of paper measuring at least 8½" by 11", students can design sheets of commemorative stamps illustrating Minhagim followed during Shabbat, Ḥanukkah, birthdays, and one more holiday of their own choosing. Designs can be cut out with a pinking shears and pasted in "Minhagim Stamp Albums," with one album per student or one for the entire class.

4. Ask each student to make up five "Ḥanukkah trivia" questions. Use (or save) the questions for a Ḥanukkah party game.

And Finally . . .

Assign "Take Five" (Student Activity Book, p. 43) for drill and review.

NOTE: The links to the "Mitzvah" chapter (text, pp. 67–74) and especially to the "Have You Heard?" on p. 72, should already be clear to you.

Answers to "Review It" Questions: p. 65: (1) by the words בְּמִצְוֹתָיו and וְצִוָּנוּ in the blessing over candle lighting; (2) the exact number of candles that must be lit; p. 66: (1) they are cooked in oil, which reminds us of the miracle of the holy oil; (2) the number value of nun, gimmel, hay, and shin equals 358, the same number value as מָשִׁיחַ, the Messiah who will lead all nations to a future time of peace and plenty.

Answers to Student Activity Book Questions: p. 42: items 3, 6, 8, and 9 should be marked as מִצְוָה, items 1 and 4 as הֲלָכָה, and items 2, 5, 7, and 10 as מִנְהָג; p. 43: (1) Jewish custom; (2) eating fish, lighting two (or seven or ten) candles, lighting a candle for each family member, etc.; (3) giving gifts at Ḥanukkah time (borrowed from Christmas); (4) because Halachah does not always spell out completely how a Mitzvah is to be fulfilled, leaving people, families, and communities free to fulfill the commandment in their own ways.

CHAPTER TEN

MITZVAH

Objectives

1. To introduce the concept of Mitzvah as commandment.

2. To show that Mitzvot should be fulfilled for their own sake and not in the expectation of a specific reward.

3. To demonstrate the importance of Mitzvot in Jewish life.

Background

The word "Mitzvah" and its variants show up frequently in Jewish life. Surely all of your students are by now at least generally familiar with the terms "Bar Mitzvah" and "Bat Mitzvah." Some of them may already recognize (or recall from p. 64 of the text) the significance of the Mitzvah-words בְּמִצְוֹתָיו and וְצִוָּנוּ in the blessing over candle lighting. Not only on Shabbat but every time we welcome a holiday or a special event with its appropriate blessing we acknowledge that God commands.

Your students are probably most familiar with the idea that "doing a Mitzvah" means doing a good deed. In this sense, fixing a flat tire on someone's bike, phoning a sick friend with the evening's homework assignment, and letting your younger brother borrow your Beatles tape might all be described as "doing a Mitzvah." Although the introductory definition (text, p. 67) recognizes this common meaning, the chapter itself is concerned almost exclusively with the more formal sense of Mitzvah as commandment. You should make this distinction clear to the class, but you should nevertheless feel free to explore with your students the question of how this association between "commandment" and "good deed" came about. Is it possible that there is some notion hidden in this mixture of meanings that *doing good things* is a commandment—as if that were the most fundamental, most natural, most essential kind of Jewish behavior?

The chapter opens (p. 69) with the assertion that, according to tradition, there are 613 Mitzvot, 365 negative and 248 positive. Chapter Fourteen (text, pp. 95–102) deals specifically with Aseret HaDibrot, the Ten Commandments. Obviously, the Ten Commandments, important as they are, form only a small part of the commandment system of the Jewish people. The Ten Commandments may be the most basic, and they may deal with the largest issues (and the ones that have compelled the most universal assent), but the commandments of Torah are many.

What, then, is the text really saying when it quotes Yehudah HaNasi (p. 71)?

Be just as careful in doing what may seem like a minor Mitzvah as you are in doing what may seem like an important Mitzvah. You do not know what the reward for each may be.

Does the text really mean to urge us to follow the commandments of Leviticus regarding sacrificial offerings, ritual cleanliness, and kashrut with as much rectitude and fervor as the commandments to observe Shabbat and refrain from murder? If the reason for observing the Ten Commandments is indeed that they were *commanded by God* (and not that they "make sense" or follow "natural law"), what reasons can be given for neglecting to obey laws that could, with equal justification, be construed as divine commandments?

This is a sensitive subject—especially sensitive if you as a teacher have difficulty with the idea that God issued any such specific commands. One way to deal with this dilemma is to acknowledge that religion is meant to challenge us, to remind us of possibilities rather than to present us with notions to which we already assent. If we are not always prepared to fulfill every commandment, we can at least make the effort to understand.

Words to the Wise

Key terms:

commandment

*Halachah

*Midrash

*Minhag

*Mitzvah (מִצְוָה), Mitzvot (מִצְוֹת)

Other terms:

negative

positive

privilege

specify

summoned

tendency

Delving into the Chapter

Read and discuss the definition of "Mitzvah" and review the definitions of "Halachah" and "Minhag." If you haven't already assigned the exercise on p. 42 of the Student Activity Book, you may wish to do so now.

Go over with the class the story of the king and the three gardeners. Ask your students:

- If someone hired you to mow the lawn or rake leaves, would you take the job without asking what the pay was? Do you think the three gardeners were wise to take the job without asking in advance about the payment? Why do you think they neglected to ask? Perhaps jobs were scarce, and they needed the work, regardless of whether the pay was generous or stingy. Could it be that they were so pleased at being hired by such a great king that they did not even bother to ask? Do you see any similarity between the king hiring the gardeners and God choosing the people of Israel to follow His commandments?

- How much did the gardener who took care of the olive tree get? What was the rate for taking care of the pepper tree? For the white-flower tree? Do you think it was fair of the king to pay the gardeners different amounts (assuming the gardeners worked equally hard)? What about the idea of "equal pay for equal work"—isn't this generally the fairest way to reward the people who work for you? On the other hand, do you agree with the king's statement that if the gardeners had known the wages in advance, all of them would have wanted to work on the olive tree, and the other two trees would have been neglected?

- In what way is the king like God? How are the Jewish people like the gardeners? Does it sometimes happen that people who work equally hard get unequal rewards? Is this fair? Would the people feel any better or work any harder if they always knew in advance what their (unequal) rewards would be?

- When asked to do something, do you usually ask "What's in it for me?" Or do you say: "I'd better do as I'm told" or "This is the right thing to do"?

To explore further the relationship between Mitzvah and reward, have the class do pp. 44–45 of the Student Activity Book.

Turning Discussion into Action. The following are some Mitzvot the students in your class can perform either individually or in a group:

(a) Adopt grandparents in a retirement home. Write them letters, bake treats for them (if their diets permit), and visit them as often as possible.

(b) Offer to prepare or organize the Oneg Shabbat after a Shabbat service. Or, if the rabbi agrees, prepare a special program for the service itself.

(c) Volunteer in the synagogue office—answer the telephone, stuff envelopes, collect Tzedakah.

(d) Read stories to a kindergarten class—or read some of your own writings to them.

(e) Make a mural for the temple. You could show Mitzvot being performed, holiday customs, or scenes from Jewish history.

Up for Discussion

1. Now let's try to connect the Mitzvahs (good deeds) with the Mitzvot (commandments) from which they spring. What's the difference between a positive and a negative commandment? Why does the Torah have more negative than positive commandments? Which are easier to carry out? Which kind of "commandment" at home would students rather receive—positive ("Take out the garbage!") or negative ("Stop teasing your baby sister!")?

2. Ask the class: What is the meaning of the expression "Virtue is its own reward"? If virtue is so rewarding, why do people misbehave? Does telling people the reasons for doing the right thing make them any more likely to do it? Does telling people the punishment for doing the *wrong* thing make them more likely to act correctly? What about offering rewards—a raise in allowance, a trip to an amusement park, a candy bar? Which of these techniques do your parents use most often? Which technique is more effective in getting you to do the right thing? Over the long term, which approach do you think is most likely to help you develop into a better person?

Write On!

1. Have each student make a list of all the Mitzvot performed in a day (e.g., studying, being respectful to parents and teachers, helping the needy, washing up in the morning). Which ones were done for a reward? Which ones were done for the pleasure of performing them? Which ones were done because someone said they absolutely had to be done?

2. Tell your students: Imagine that you have died and have been summoned before God, Who challenges you to call three witnesses to tell Him how good a person you've been. Write a brief play including your dialogue with God and what the three witnesses have to say about you. (Hint: The witnesses don't have to be people. They could be pets or toys or objects—even, as in the story, your good deeds.)

3. Do your students always accept "commandments" from their parents without question? Have each student write at least two paragraphs explaining the answer. What are the good points and bad points about obeying orders unquestioningly? Encourage your students to give concrete examples. Reinforce this exercise with p. 46 of the Student Activity Book.

And Finally . . .

Assign "Take Five" (Student Activity Book, p. 47) for review or diagnostic testing.

Answers to "Review It" Questions: p. 72: (1) if the rewards for Mitzvot were specified, we would, like the gardeners, tend to do those Mitzvot whose rewards were great and neglect those whose rewards were small; p. 74: (1) while the family can see to a proper burial, the Mitzvot a person does speak well of him long after his death.

Answers to Student Activity Book Questions: p. 47: (1) a commandment; a good deed; (2) the number of days in a year (365) plus the number of parts of the human body (248) = the number of negative plus positive Mitzvot = 613; (3) the privilege of doing another Mitzvah; (4) they stay with you, speak well of you, give you enjoyment, make you feel good, etc.

CHAPTER ELEVEN

NEVI'IM

Objectives

1. To introduce Nevi'im as the second section of the Tanach, from which the weekly Haftarah passage is selected.

2. To portray the Navi as someone who speaks for God.

3. To summarize the basic ideas of the Nevi'im, notably their commitment to social justice.

Background

The chapter employs the word "Nevi'im" in two distinct senses: as one of the three parts of the Tanach, and as a Hebrew name for an extraordinary group of people we call "prophets." Nevi'im has many books, and it would be folly to expect your students to remember all their names, either in English or in Hebrew. Nevertheless, the class should be able to grasp the link between Nevi'im and Haftarah, and to recognize that a Haftarah reading from Jeremiah or Isaiah or Amos comes from Nevi'im.

It's customary to begin a discussion of the Nevi'im as people who speak for God by contrasting this distinctly Hebraic concept with the contemporary idea of the "prophet" as a soothsayer or fortune teller or astrologer—someone able to read palms, puzzle out tea leaves, or gaze into a crystal ball and divine the future. Presumably your students are familiar with this sense of "prophet," but are they perfectly clear about the meaning of "spokesman"?

A spokesperson, obviously, is someone who speaks for someone else: you might try the analogy of the presidential press secretary, who speaks to the press when the president does not wish to address the public directly. We assume the press secretary enjoys the president's full confidence, else the president would surely replace him. But in the case of the Navi, how do we know the spokesperson speaks on the proper authority and conveys the proper message? The fact is that in each Navi's own time there were contrary claimants, those whom the Nevi'im denounced as "false prophets." How do we know who were the true prophets and who were the false? By tradition, which is another word for hindsight: the unrighteous *were* punished, the wicked *did* fall, the people *were* exiled, the exiles *were* redeemed, ethical Judaism survived, and both the priesthood and its Temple rituals vanished. Such is the verdict of history, but in their own time those who listened to the Nevi'im had no such assurance.

The two definitions of "Nevi'im" make an interesting contrast. To put the matter succinctly: Not every Navi is in Nevi'im, and not everyone in Nevi'im is a Navi. The second half of the conundrum is obvious, for every Navi must have his audience, every Nathan his David. The first half is proved by the chapter itself, which spotlights Moses as the first and greatest of the Nevi'im. Your class should recognize that the story of Moses' life is contained wholly within the Torah (or Ḥumash), not Nevi'im.

The chapter discusses the personalities of the Nevi'im chiefly in terms of their reluctance to speak (though not every Navi showed such hesitation) and their commitment to social justice. Did all the Nevi'im concentrate on improving the welfare of the poor and the disadvantaged? The answer is no, but in the case of those who did, you have an excellent opportunity to convey to your class the concerns the Jewish tradition shows for the welfare of all people.

The reluctance of some Nevi'im to speak is a somewhat more abstract issue, but one which may nevertheless be of interest to your students. Who among us finds it easy to speak out against our fellow citizens? Who among us feels comfortable denouncing those of greater wealth, power, or outward piety? What does it feel like to believe that God has commanded you to follow such a risky and unpopular course? How can the Navi know the difference between conscience or dream or delusion and the true voice of God? How can you know when someone is truly speaking for God or is merely mouthing words for his or her personal benefit?

The chapter offers a good opportunity not only for your students to learn about Nevi'im but also for you to refresh your own knowledge of the prophetic books. You might want to consult two excellent modern commentaries: *The Prophets*, by Abraham Joshua Heschel, and the sections on Nevi'im in *The Hebrew Scriptures*, by Samuel Sandmel. Sandmel's presentation is more straightforward, whereas Heschel's is more inspirational. The *Encyclopaedia Judaica* has informative articles on each of the prophetic books and under the heading "Prophets and Prophecy."

A famous essay known as "Priest and Prophet," by the modern Jewish thinker Aḥad HaAm, appears in translation in many places and is definitely worth your attention. Aḥad HaAm's by now familiar distinction between the two types of leaders in religious communities can be very helpful in guiding your own understanding of the different tasks of religious leadership within Judaism. The two main roles are, roughly, those of the priestly leaders, charged with carrying out Judaism's ceremonial functions, and the prophetic tradition, with its impulse to challenge authority and ceremony in the interests of a more just social order. Though the distinction is not perfectly clean, it does help shed some light on the religious tasks that face all of us who care about the Jewish tradition.

Words to the Wise

Key terms:

*Haftarah

*Nevi'im (נְבִיאִים), Navi (נָבִיא)

Pharaoh

prophet

spokesman, spokesmen

*Tanach

Books of the Nevi'im (in order):

EARLY PROPHETS	נְבִיאִים רִאשׁוֹנִים
Joshua	יְהוֹשֻׁעַ
Judges	שׁוֹפְטִים
I Samuel	שְׁמוּאֵל א
II Samuel	שְׁמוּאֵל ב
I Kings	מְלָכִים א
II Kings	מְלָכִים ב
LATER PROPHETS	נְבִיאִים אַחֲרוֹנִים
Isaiah	יְשַׁעְיָה
Jeremiah	יִרְמְיָה
Ezekiel	יְחֶזְקֵאל
TWELVE MINOR PROPHETS	תְּרֵי—עָשָׂר
Hosea	הוֹשֵׁעַ
Joel	יוֹאֵל
Amos	עָמוֹס
Obadiah	עוֹבַדְיָה
Jonah	יוֹנָה
Micah	מִיכָה
Nahum	נַחוּם
Habakkuk	חֲבַקּוּק
Zephaniah	צְפַנְיָה
Haggai	חַגַּי
Zechariah	זְכַרְיָה
Malachi	מַלְאָכִי

Other terms:

conscience

rebellion

reluctant

Yigdal

Delving into the Chapter

If the class has already studied the "Ḥumash" and "Ketuvim" chapters (text, pp. 23–30, 31–38), you can assign Duplicating Master #8 ("Ḥumash, Nevi'im, Ketuvim") for this chapter or use it as the basis for a challenging—and nontrivial—game of "Torah Pursuit."

Go over the introductory material (text, pp. 75–77), taking care to distinguish the two main senses of "Nevi'im." Have the text of *Yigdal* available for study. Teach the hymn if the class doesn't know it already.

Use the story of Moses and the burning bush as a way of getting into the whole issue of the reluctant prophet. Draw on your own childhood experiences as you ask your students:

- What are some things your parents ask you to do around the house? (Clean up your room, wash the dishes, take out the garbage, walk the dog, etc.)

- Do you always do what your parents ask as soon as they ask you? Or do you sometimes postpone the things you're asked to do? When you do postpone something, what kinds of reasons or excuses do you give? (Don't feel well, too busy, have to go over to a friend's house, etc.) Do you try to get your parents to ask someone else—say, one of your sisters or brothers? How do your parents respond to these excuses?

■ What did God ask Moses to do? What did God ask Jeremiah to do? How did Moses and Jeremiah answer? What kinds of excuses did Moses and Jeremiah offer? How did God respond? The Navi Nathan acted as David's conscience—who acted as Moses' conscience?

For an extreme example of a reluctant prophet, review the story of Jonah (text, pp. 17–19). "Banner Days" (Student Activity Book, p. 48) provides a creative exercise based on the lives of Moses, Jonah, and Jeremiah.

Up for Discussion

1. What does a prophet do? What kind of message does a prophet deliver? In order for a prophet to be a spokesman *for* God, is it necessary that God address the prophet directly? Or could anyone who preaches the message of justice and Torah be considered a prophet? The rabbis of the Talmud thought that the prophetic age—the period of divine inspiration—had ceased several centuries before the Roman era. Does the class think any prophets might be alive today? If so, does anyone want to offer a nomination? What about some people from the American past: Martin Luther King, Jr.? Abraham Lincoln? Thomas Jefferson?

For more on the possibility of prophecy today, see p. 49 of the Student Activity Book.

2. Read together with the class II Samuel 11–12. Stage a "trial" of David based on the Biblical text. Let Nathan act as prosecutor, calling as witnesses Bathsheba and Joab—perhaps even the ghost of Uriah! After Nathan's summation, David should be allowed to make a statement of contrition.

3. The Nevi'im often contrasted ritual with righteousness, reflecting a time when the roles of priest and prophet were almost wholly at odds. Today, however, the rabbi in a typical congregation carries the burden of being both "priest" and "prophet," superintending both ritual matters and the temple's program of Tzedakah and Tikkun Olam. Invite the rabbi in to discuss how his/her role contrasts with (or combines) the roles of priest and prophet in ancient times. Does your rabbi sense any tension between the two?

Write On!

1. Topics for special reports, written and/or oral:
   (a) Relations between Moses and Aaron;
   (b) Miriam as a prophet;
   (c) Theories about the "burning bush";
   (d) The life of Jeremiah;
   (e) The influence of the Nevi'im on Islam.

2. Ask your students: In school, at home, at camp, or in a club, have you ever held an unpopular point of view that other people tried to argue you out of? Did you stick with your opinion? Did you change it? Have students write at least two paragraphs describing the problem and how the situation was resolved.

3. Present the concept of cause and effect to the class. Point out how the Nevi'im perceived a cause-and-effect relationship between misbehavior and punishment, and between repentance and reward. Then assign "Cause and Effect" (Duplicating Master #9).

And Finally . . .

"Make the Message Clear" (Student Activity Book, p. 50) is a simple word scramble that can provide a lively introduction to more serious topics. Use "Take Five" (p. 51) for reinforcement and review.

NOTE: The numerous links between the chapters on Humash, Ketuvim, Nevi'im, and Tanach have already been mentioned. The next chapter, "Sefer Torah" (text, pp. 83–88), like the earlier "Mezuzah" (pp. 53–60), focuses on a ritual object rather than on abstract ideas. Consider planning a session with the rabbi that would allow students to have a closeup view of the Sefer Torah and its ornaments. If you live near a major urban area, a visit to a Sofer may also be possible.

Answers to "Review It" Questions: p. 80: (1) God called on them to be His spokesman, God assured them He was with them, they responded reluctantly, they claimed to be poor speakers; (2) Moses was to lead the Israelites to freedom, whereas Jeremiah was to warn the people that if they didn't mend their ways, they would lose their freedom; p. 82: (1) God would punish them; (2) d.

Answers to Student Activity Book Questions: p. 50: THE TEMPLE WILL BE DESTROYED, INJUSTICE WILL LEAD TO PUNISHMENT, PURSUE JUSTICE AND HELP THOSE IN NEED, WHEN GOD CALLS THE NAVI ANSWERS; p. 51: (1) prophet *or* spokesman for God; (2) foretell the future; the ancient Hebrew meaning is "one who speaks for God"; (3) Moses; (4) Moses said he couldn't speak clearly; Jeremiah said he was only a child.

Answers to Questions on Duplicating Master #8: 2, 8, 11, and 16 should be labeled ח; 4, 6, 7, 13, 18 and 20 should be labeled ג; and 1, 3, 5, 10, 12, 15, and 19 should be labeled כ.

CHAPTER TWELVE

SEFER TORAH

Objectives

1. To show how the Sefer Torah is inscribed and decorated.
2. To explain why all texts of the Sefer Torah must be as alike as possible.

Background

Most of *Basic Judaism for Young People: Torah* deals with ideas and literature rather than with objects. But in Jewish life some objects are of such central importance that they take on an aura of holiness. This is most certainly true of the Sefer Torah and the Holy Ark in which it is kept.

Jews, sometimes called the "people of the Book," have always accorded books—especially bound volumes of the sacred texts—particular honor. (The *Israel* volume has an entire chapter, "Am HaSefer," devoted to this phenomenon.) Books, however, may be shelved in a library, stacked on a desk, stashed in a cabinet, or packed in a bookbag; only the Sefer Torah has its own special home, the Holy Ark, or Aron Ha-Kodesh, which unlike a bookshelf or briefcase is itself an object of reverence. Words of Torah may be written, typed, tape recorded, computer coded, expanded, paraphrased, or abridged. The Sefer Torah, on the other hand, has been inscribed in the same way for century after century—written on parchment, not typing paper, with a quill pen, not a ballpoint, copied by a Sofer and not by a Xerox machine. The Sefer Torah links us not only with the wisdom of our ancestors but also with the spirit and technology of an earlier age. Rashi, were he to appear today, would be dumfounded to see the phosphorescent glow of Torah on a computer monitor, but he would instantly recognize the Sefer Torah, and he would handle it with a reverence that would be clearly recognizable to us.

Writing a Sefer Torah is a difficult business, involving people whose lives resemble very little those of the students you are likely to teach. This may pose a dilemma for you, but it may also be an opportunity for you to tap some of your own creativity. In a world where we tend to take fine things for granted, or assume that handwork is a dying art, the tradition of the Sofer insists that every step and every product reflect painstaking attention and care.

Words to the Wise

Key terms:

breastplate

*Ḥumash

kosher

mantle

*Midrash

parchment

rimmonim

scribe

*Sefer Torah (סֵפֶר תּוֹרָה), Sifrei Torah (סִפְרֵי תּוֹרָה)

*Sofer (סוֹפֵר), Sofrim (סוֹפְרִים)

watchword

Other terms:

adornments

eternal

pumice stone

reverence

Delving into the Chapter

This chapter can't really be a "hands on" experience: as the caption on p. 108 of the text indicates, the yad was introduced to ensure that human hands would not touch the holy Torah parchment. But with the rabbi's help, you can arrange for your class to enter the sanctuary and examine the Sefer Torah at close range. Make sure your students can identify each of the ornaments, observe the crowned letters and stitched parchment seams, and—if the scroll is turned to Deuteronomy 6:4—get a good look at the enlarged ayin and dalet of the Shema.

If you live near a major metropolitan area, you may be able to arrange a visit with a Sofer. If not, you may still be able to find a member of the congregation or community well versed in the scribal arts and willing to show your class some of the elements of Hebrew calligraphy. The exercises on pp. 52–54 of the Student Activity Book, along with Duplicating Master #10, simulate both the tasks of the Sofer and the creative joy of Hiddur Mitzvah.

Up for Discussion

1. Ask your students: What benefits does Judaism gain from the fact that the text of every Sefer Torah must be inscribed in exactly the same way? What benefits derive from the fact that each Sefer Torah may be decorated differently? If your class has studied the "Mezuzah" chapter (pp. 53–60), draw an analogy between the Mezuzah case and the Torah ornaments. If you didn't introduce the concept of Hiddur Mitzvah earlier, now is the time to do so (see p. 31 of this Teacher's Guide).

2. What is reverence? How do we show our reverence and respect for a beloved relative or teacher? Have your students name some people they revere and tell why. To which objects do Jews show reverence? (Sefer Torah, Mezuzah, tallit, prayerbooks, etc.) Since a person has feelings but an object doesn't, why should we bother to show our reverence toward it? (Not necessarily for what the object is but for what it represents.) Are there any secular objects to which we show reverence? (The national flag and great works of art stand out among many possible answers.) How do we express our reverence for them?

3. A Sefer Torah is very expensive to buy or repair—why? Discuss with the class the concept of mass production and the effect it has on quality. You might want to make a comparison with automobiles: the production-line Chevrolet may be a good car at a good price, but it cannot match the one-of-a-kind quality of the much more costly Rolls-Royce. Try to draw analogous examples from the students' own experience, e.g., a personalized sweater knit by a favorite relative vs. a machine-knit sweater that came off the production line with thousands of others. Toward which sweater are your students more likely to show a sentimental attachment?

Write On!

1. Assign students to research the origins of the Aron HaKodesh, Torah mantle, crown, breastplate, binder, and yad. Have them report to the class on their findings. These reports could be timed to coincide with the session with the rabbi in the sanctuary with the Sefer Torah.

2. You can base a lesson on the history of writing by assigning special reports on (a) cuneiform, (b) calligraphy, (c) papyrus, (d) parchment, (e) printing, and (f) bookbinding.

3. Have students prepare lists of specific questions they would ask a Sofer in a talk-show interview about his work. You can then simulate the talk show, allowing students to take turns being Sofer or interviewer.

4. Choose a holiday (if one is upcoming) or an important event in the Bible and discuss it with the class, roughing out the story as you go. Divide your students into several small groups and have each group write one "panel" on that topic. After each group has finished its draft, distribute sections of a roll of shelf paper and have each group write down and illustrate its portion of the story. Stress the idea that this job must be perfect and contain no mistakes. (Better have some shelf paper in reserve, just in case.) When all the portions have been finished, fasten the shelf paper together and make a scroll, which can then be tied with a ribbon and stored in a special place in the classroom. Members of your class may enjoy showing the scroll to younger students, or perhaps the scroll can be shared at a holiday service.

And Finally...

"Take Five" (Student Activity Book, p. 55) provides an occasion for review or diagnostic testing.

NOTE: An excursion to the sanctuary to examine the Sefer Torah provides a natural bridge to the "Aliyah" chapter which follows (pp. 89–94).

Answers to "Review It" Questions: p. 87 (1) to make sure he is transcribing the Torah text exactly; he must use black ink, parchment from a kosher animal, thread from the muscles of a kosher animal, never erase the name of God, etc.; p. 88 (1) because vowels were not added until centuries after the death of Moses; (2) the Midrash about עַיִן; the Midrash about אֶחָד and אַחֵר.

Answers to Student Activity Book Questions: p. 55; (1) scribe; (2) parchment; (3) decorating the Sefer Torah with beautiful ornaments, rising when the Sefer Torah is removed from the Holy Ark, kissing the Sefer Torah as it is carried through the sanctuary; (4) g, c, e, d, a, f, b; (5) because Moses told the Israelites to "observe everything that I command you, without adding anything or taking anything away."

CHAPTER THIRTEEN

ALIYAH

Objectives

1. To understand Aliyah as the honor of being called to the bimah to recite the blessings before and after the Torah reading.

2. To discuss the connection between Aliyah in the Torah service and Aliyah as immigration to Israel.

3. To outline the traditional steps in receiving an Aliyah.

4. To describe the important occasions that call for special Aliyot.

Background

This chapter demonstrates the way in which something that might be considered routine becomes special because of the attitude of the participants. You might want to point out some analogies in the lives of your students. Birthdays, for example, are really an annual routine, and yet on the anniversary of one's birth, the person honored by a party or by special gifts feels anything but routine. Each year, at the end of summer, millions of children enter new schools or new grades with different teachers. Routine, yes, but also exciting, and—your students may admit—often a little scary.

So it is with an Aliyah. Anyone who is capable of reciting the appropriate blessing and who meets the established congregational qualifications is capable of an Aliyah, and in the course of time will likely receive one. Yet, on the day when one is so designated, the congregant is likely to feel a tingle of elation and perhaps even trepidation. Coming so directly into the presence of Torah is itself a source of heightened awareness. On this occasion, too, an anxious adult worshiper, especially one making a rare appearance at services, may find reason to doubt whether he or she is really a "good Jew" and to fear that fumbling the Aliyah will make his or her inadequacies plain to the entire congregation. On the other hand, adults often experience Aliyah as part of a simḥa in which the honor of being called to the Torah mingles with the pleasure and pride of the occasion—most often the Bar or Bat Mitzvah of a beloved family member.

Aliyot can be given on any number of special occasions, including the ones cited in the text. But a person may also request an opportunity to recite a blessing over the Torah because of personal feelings or life-cycle events. Some congregations allocate the Aliyot on the High Holy Days to those who have given exceptional service to the congregation, as a way of honoring them.

The connection between the two meanings of Aliyah—immigration to Israel and the recitation of Torah blessings—is suggestive. We suspect that neither theme bulks large in the daily lives of most Jewish fourth- and fifth-graders in North America, but with a little imagination you can help forge this link in the minds of your students. Children at this age are beginning to think of their Bar or Bat Mitzvah ceremonies and the fact that they will soon be qualified for Aliyot. At the same time, the notion of a new life in a new land may also appeal to them because of the independence and brave outlook it represents. The connections between responsibility and freedom and between spiritual values and personal opportunity are ones your students should be able to grasp.

Words to the Wise

Key terms:

*Aliyah (עֲלִיָה), Aliyot (עֲלִיוֹת)

bimah (בִּימָה)

*Haftarah (הַפְטָרָה)

*Maftir (מַפְטִיר)

*Midrash

*Minhag, Minhagim

Simḥat Torah

tallit

Other terms:

bridegroom

congregation

fruitfulness

traditional

Delving into the Chapter

Like "Sefer Torah" (text, pp. 83–88), this chapter offers an excellent opportunity to bring your class into the sanctuary for some firsthand experience of Jewish worship. Think of the bimah as a stage and the text on pp. 91–93 as a kind of drama. If possible, each child in the class should be called up to recite the Torah blessings, with the remaining class members functioning as the congregation. You may want to ask the rabbi to discuss with the class the Minhagim for reading the Torah in your synagogue.

Familiarity with Hebrew names is the theme of the "Family Album" exercise in the Student Activity Book (pp. 56–57); in "Up on the Bimah" (p. 58), students are asked to schedule the Aliyot for their Bar or Bat Mitzvah.

Up for Discussion

1. Why is it an honor to be called up to read from the Torah? Encourage students to compare the reverence the congregation shows the Torah through Aliyot with the reverence a Sofer shows in writing a Sefer Torah. (This activity presumes that the class has already studied the "Sefer Torah" chapter.)

2. Who should have the honor of an Aliyah? Suppose the class were to start its own small synagogue. Should every congregant be given the opportunity—or required—to have an individual Aliyah at least once a year? Or should the Aliyot be used to honor those who have done the most for the synagogue and the Jewish community? Should men and women share equally in receiving Aliyot? When should children be allowed to have an Aliyah? Should the person called to the bimah be required to read the Torah blessings in Hebrew (or in transliteration)? Or should English be allowed?

Write On!

1. Assign students to write at least two paragraphs using any one of these starters:
   - When I am called up to read the Torah ...
   - Receiving an Aliyah is an honor because ...
   - My Bar (or Bat) Mitzvah will be special to me because ...
   - If I decided to move to Israel ...

2. Have the class create storyboards or strip cartoons illustrating each of the steps in receiving an Aliyah.

And Finally ...

"The Choice Is Yours" (Student Activity Book, p. 59) and "Take Five" (p. 60) provide opportunities for review and testing.

NOTE: In discussing the special group Aliyah given to children in some congregations on Simḥat Torah, you may wish to refer to the story in the "Torah" chapter (text, pp. 119–120). You might want to follow up "Aliyah" with the "Parashat HaShavua" chapter (pp. 103–08), which discusses the origins of the ritual of Torah reading.

Answers to "Review It" Questions: p. 93: (1) (a) the Torah teaches us the truth, (b) God has planted everlasting life in our midst, (c) may you grow in strength; (2) to show that you are not anxious to leave the Torah; p. 94: (1) Simḥat Torah.

Answers to Student Activity Book Questions: p. 59: (1) b, (2) c, (3) a, (4) a, (5) b; p. 60: (1) the act of going up, being called to the bimah to recite the Torah blessings, immigration to Israel; (3) Bar or Bat Mitzvah, birth of a child, marriage, Simḥat Torah; (4) Simḥat Torah; (5) h, a, g, c, e, b, d, i, f.

Answers to Duplicating Master #11: The four occasions are BAR (or BAT) MITZVAH, MARRIAGE, SHABBAT, and SIMḤAT TORAH.

CHAPTER FOURTEEN

ASERET HADIBROT

Objectives

1. To familiarize students with the Ten Commandments in their Biblical sequence (Exodus 20:2–14).

2. To show how the first commandment can be interpreted as the commandment to be free.

3. To convey the joy many Jews feel in obeying the fourth commandment, to observe and remember Shabbat.

4. To demonstrate how covetousness, which is prohibited by the tenth commandment, can lead to violations of other commandments.

Background

No one would deny that the Ten Commandments have been fundamental to the development of Western law, ethics, and religion. They are the shared heritage of Jews and Christians alike, and they can be seen as a kind of blueprint for human behavior from which other, more detailed guides may be said to flow. The Ten Commandments speak to our relationships with God, with our families, with our fellow creatures, and with our own potentialities for good or evil.

Because of their widespread acceptance as foundation stones of Western behavior, the Ten Commandments have been the occasion for important works of art. (Depictions of Aseret HaDibrot appear on p. 90 and p. 96 of the text.) Because Moses is twice portrayed in the Bible as coming down from the mountain with the tablets of the Law, artists throughout history have often depicted him in this role. Many people are familiar with the idea that Moses broke the tablets of Aseret HaDibrot in fury over the people's building the Golden Calf as an idol in his absence, and that—according to one tradition—he was later punished for his anger.

Even as we pay tribute to the power and influence of Aseret HaDibrot, however, we must also recognize how much of authentic Jewish experience stands outside the framework of the Ten Commandments. Of all the holy days and rituals, only Shabbat receives a mention. The concepts of Aggadah, Haftarah, Ketuvim, Leshon HaKodesh, Midrash, Mezuzah, Minhag, Nevi'im, Sefer Torah, Aliyah, Parashat HaShavua, Talmud, and Tanach—all these and many more essential Jewish ideas find no place in the Ten Commandments. The truth is that Aseret HaDibrot, given to and/or adopted by an ancient people who led simple lives, make up only a small part of the legislation and traditions that have historically defined what it means to be a Jew. In the Biblical passages that immediately follow Aseret HaDibrot, many more laws (מִשְׁפָּטִים) are spelled out, establishing specific requirements for civil as well as ritual behavior. Your students may recall from the opening of the "Mitzvah" chapter (text, p. 69) that Jewish tradition credits the Torah with not ten but 613 Mitzvot. Today many of us tend to classify the Mitzvot as major or minor (with Aseret HaDibrot as the "top ten"), but the Torah makes no such distinction.

Words to the Wise

Key terms:	*Other terms:*
*Aggadah	bondage
*Aseret HaDibrot (עֲשֶׂרֶת הַדִּבְּרוֹת)	oppressed
commandment	vineyard
covet, coveting	violation
Havdalah	
*Nevi'im	

Delving into the Chapter

After reviewing with your students the introductory definition (text, p. 95) and the form in which Aseret HaDibrot are usually depicted, you can point out to the class that the Ten Commandments appear not once but twice in the Torah: at Exodus 20:2–14 and Deuteronomy 5:6–18. You might want to photocopy both versions in English and have students compare them, noting especially the differences between the two versions of commandments four and ten. Use the chalkboard to enumerate and summarize the commandments, and encourage the students to classify each commandment under the headings "Obligations to God" or "Obligations to Other People." Discuss with the class the ways in which the fifth commandment serves as a bridge between the two groups.

You can use the exercise on p. 61 of the Student Activity Book to reinforce this lesson.

Up for Discussion

1. The text points out why the first commandment, which doesn't tell us to do anything specific, is nevertheless a commandment. But why is it the *first* commandment? In what sense do all the commandments flow from the acknowledgment of God? Why is the commandment to be free the most basic of all the commandments? Aren't all the subsequent, more specific obligations meaningless unless each of us has the freedom to choose good or evil?

2. Why is the fifth commandment to honor our parents just as important as honoring God? In what ways can God be considered our parent? The Student Activity Book (p. 62) offers an exercise on this theme.

3. Suppose the Ten Commandments had never existed, and there were no laws against lying, stealing, and killing. What would the world be like? Would people be more free—or less? If there were no laws, could there still be order? If so, who would maintain it? Would any of your students prefer living in such a world to the one we have now?

4. Many Western religions regard the Ten Commandments as a sound basis for behavior. Could you obey all the Ten Commandments and still not be a good person? Conversely, could you be a good person and not obey the Ten Commandments? Are there important aspects of ethical behavior that Aseret HaDibrot leave out? What about regular worship? Charity? Behaving toward others in a cheerful and kindly manner?

Write On!

1. Some years ago there was a popular song called "The Ten Commandments of Love." Have students compose ten commandments for (a) being a good friend, (b) being a good student, (c) being a star athlete, (d) being a good parent, or (e) an even better topic of your own devising. You might want to make this assignment after students have completed the "Positive and Negative Mitzvot" exercise on p. 63 of the Student Activity Book.

2. Have students write at least two paragraphs using one of these starters:
- If no one obeyed the Ten Commandments . . .
- If everyone always obeyed the Ten Commandments . . .
- If I could add an eleventh commandment . . .
- If I could abolish one of the Ten Commandments . . .
- Honoring our parents is not always easy because . . .

3. Assign students to write articles for the "Torah Times." Each article should include the who, what, where, when, and why of the event and a headline that conveys the story's key idea. Assignments might include King David's dealings with Uriah and Bathsheba, and Moses' smashing of the tablets when he sees the Golden Calf. If you have the time and energy, you can guide your students in producing their own class newspaper.

And Finally . . .

Assign "Take Five" (Student Activity Book, p. 64) for reinforcement and review.

NOTE: A nontrivial game of "Torah Pursuit" that focuses on identifying the commandments and recalling their order can be expanded to include review of key names and concepts from other chapters.

Answers to "Review It" Questions: p. 99: (1) by reminding us that God freed us from slavery in Egypt; p. 100: (1) the son was rude to him and showed him no respect; (2) the people were not acting properly; p. 102: (1) Ahab and Naboth—tenth, ninth, sixth, eighth; David and Uriah—tenth, sixth, seventh.

Answers to Student Activity Book Questions: p. 64: (1) עֲשֶׂרֶת הַדִּבְּרוֹת; (2) "I am the Lord your God, Who brought you out of the land of Egypt, out of the house of bondage"; it's a statement rather than a specific obligation; (3) Shabbat, fourth; (4) murder, adultery, theft, lying, envy.

CHAPTER FIFTEEN

PARASHAT HASHAVUA

Objectives

1. To introduce Parashat HaShavua as the practice of reading the Torah according to an annual cycle of 54 portions.

2. To explain how the Torah came to be read publicly on Mondays, Thursdays, and Saturdays.

3. To demonstrate the role played by Ezra in establishing the Torah as the "constitution" of the Jewish people.

Background

Few of our children have any personal experience of reading the Torah portion on a weekly basis. But many of them are familiar with the idea of cycles—hours of the day, days of the week, seasons of the year—so the concept of a *cycle of readings* should not be difficult for your students to grasp. Nor is Parashat HaShavua the only important cycle in Jewish life. Linked to the cycle of Torah readings is the cycle of Haftarah readings and the annual round of Jewish holy days. Brit, Bar/Bat Mitzvah, wedding, and funeral are Jewish life-cycle events most students are well aware of.

Although much research has been devoted to the question of when the practice of Parashat HaShavua originated, we are still not certain precisely when or how the command to assemble the people every seven years (Deuteronomy 31:10–13) gave way to the custom of reading the Torah in public three times a week. The chapter treats an annual cycle of 54 portions as the norm, but that is not the only cycle practiced today. Whereas Orthodox Jews adhere firmly to the Babylonian Jewish tradition of a yearly cycle, an increasing number of Reform and Conservative synagogues have adopted the triennial cycle of Torah readings, reflecting the division of the masoretic text into 154 *sedarim*. Other traditions divide the Torah in different ways, with the number of portions ranging up to 175.

What benefits does the practice of Parashat HaShavua provide? Just as the cycles of nature give structure and continuity to our daily lives, so the cycle of Parashat HaShavua lends structure and continuity to Jewish observance. The knowledge that, every Shabbat, synagogues throughout the world are reading the same Torah portion reinforces the links that Jews of different countries and cultures feel with each other. Year after year, as our lives branch out along new paths, we find new lessons in the old texts: passages that may once have seemed cold and remote are suddenly kindled with new meaning, brought out perhaps by the rabbi's sermon or Torah commentary. The practice of reading the Torah one or more times a week gives an opportunity for many members of the congregation to become active participants in the service by opening and closing the ark, removing and replacing the Sefer Torah, undressing and dressing the scroll, and reciting the Torah blessings. Congregations that complement Parashat HaShavua with an annual cycle of Haftarah readings both augment the experience of worship and increase the opportunity for the worshipers to participate.

From Parashat HaShavua stems the practice of regular scriptural readings in Catholic and Protestant churches. For any tradition that reveres the Bible, reading the text in regular cycles is an important way to keep everyone familiar with the material.

Words to the Wise

Key terms:

*Aggadah

*Ḥumash

*Parashat HaShavua (פָּרָשַׁת הַשָּׁבוּעַ), Parashah

portion

scribe

Sukkot (סֻכּוֹת)

Delving into the Chapter

You can develop the key concept of a *cycle* by having the class do the exercise on p. 65 of the Student Activity Book; follow up with Duplicating Master #12. Use these activities as a springboard for discussion:

- What are some advantages of repeating a cycle regularly? (It establishes a sense of continuity, it gives us something to look forward to, it provides stability and dependability, it lessens the temptation to leave anything out, etc.)
- Can you think of any disadvantages? (Everything is predictable, no "surprises," the routine can get boring, things are done by rote and without true feeling, etc.)
- How can we provide for freshness and spontaneity while preserving the security and dependability that a regular cycle provides? Explore with your students the ways they bring variety to the cycles of daily life. How can the Torah service benefit from the same mixture of spontaneity and routine?

Up for Discussion

1. What happens immediately after we finish reading the last Torah portion on Simḥat Torah? (We begin reading the first Parashah, בְּרֵאשִׁית.) What other practices make Simḥat Torah a special day? (Flags, banners, Torah procession, group Aliyah for children, etc.) In what ways is Simḥat Torah like a birthday party for the Torah?

2. In what ways is the Torah like water? (For another comparison of the Torah with water, see the "Torah" chapter, pp. 120–22 of the text.) Challenge your students to think of other comparisons that might express their feelings about the Torah. In what ways is the Torah like the sun, a good friend, a loving parent, a school, the air, a TV set, a flower, etc.?

For more on comparing Torah to water, see "Lifesavers" on p. 66 of the Student Activity Book.

Write On!

1. "If Moses had not lived first, God would have chosen Ezra to deliver the Torah to the people of Israel." Show the class examples of the "Help Wanted" ads that appear in any Sunday newspaper. Now ask your students to write a "want ad" for someone to give the Torah to the Israelites. What kind of job is it? What kind of qualifications would God expect the applicant to have?

Alternatively, explain to the class what a letter of recommendation is and what kind of information it usually contains. Then ask your students to address to God a letter recommending Moses, Ezra, Abraham, Esther, or some other worthy Jew for the task of delivering the Torah to Israel.

2. Assign a group of students to write a playlet in which Ezra comes into their synagogue and observes a Simḥat Torah celebration. How would the customs observed in the synagogue differ from those of the Torah readings Ezra instituted?

3. Topics for special reports:
   (a) The life of Ezra
   (b) The career of Nehemiah
   (c) The triennial cycle.

And Finally . . .

"Parashat HaShavua Word Search" (Student Activity Book, p. 67) and "Take Five" (p. 68) provide the occasion for review and testing.

NOTE: The next chapter in the text is "Rashi" (pp. 109–14). If you are organizing the course thematically, you may wish to proceed directly to "Torah" (pp. 115–22).

Answers to "Review It" Questions: p. 106: (1) according to the Midrash, Torah, like water, is present everywhere on earth, is necessary for life, and can cleanse and revive us; (2) according to the Aggadah, Moses went up Mount Sinai to receive the Torah on a Thursday and returned to the people on a Monday; Saturday was chosen because it is Shabbat; p. 108: (1) since the days of Joshua; (2) Monday and Thursday were market days, and Ezra wanted the people to use their Shabbat leisure wisely.

Answers to Student Activity Book Questions: p. 65: (3) Brit, Bar/Bat Mitzvah, marriage, funeral; p. 68: (1) portion of the week; (2) 54; (3) Moses; (4) Monday, Thursday, Saturday.

CHAPTER SIXTEEN

RASHI

Objectives

1. To portray Rashi (1040–1105 C.E.) as the most popular and influential commentator on the Ḥumash.

2. To show how Rashi's comments help improve our understanding of specific episodes in the Ḥumash.

3. To retell a famous legend concerning the circumstances of Rashi's birth, and thus to understand how legends develop.

Background

Like so many figures in Jewish lore, Rashi belongs to both history and legend. You can do a lot with the fact that Rashi was a wine grower, and your students may be delighted to know that the champagne grapes which Rashi grew are still cultivated in that region of France. What is important about the portrayal of Rashi as vintner as well as scholar is that he was an intensely practical man who applied the same combination of knowledge and common sense to Torah learning as he did to earning a livelihood. He did not divorce study and worship from daily life but instead allowed insights drawn from each realm to deepen his understanding of the other. Troyes played a formative role in Rashi's outlook, since as a crossroads of commerce it offered Rashi ample opportunity to encounter many skills, disciplines and cultures. We should also remember that this period, prior to the calamitous First Crusade (1096–99), was one in which Ashkenazic Jewish traders successfully bridged the worlds between Christianity and Islam.

Rashi is hardly unique in being a figure of legend as well as fact; in this respect, he joins such American heroes as George Washington, Abraham Lincoln, and Babe Ruth, among many others. In legend, Rashi testifies to the extraordinary value invested in scholarship by Jewish tradition, and to the belief that a sound understanding of Tanach and Talmud is compatible both with an acceptance of modern life and with a willingness to interpret the scriptures in a way that reveals their relevance to contemporary experience. Young Orthodox Jews often describe their Torah study as "Ḥumash with Rashi," as though the thousand years of history that separate us from Rashi and that separates Rashi from the Biblical text were but an eyeblink.

You might want to keep in mind that the Jewish texts have had many such interpreters. Although Rashi is considered the commentator par excellence, the fact that there have been many other commentators establishes the centrality of interpretation and exegesis in the Jewish experience. The process goes on today, even in your own classroom—anywhere, indeed, that anyone reads and seeks to understand, within the context of Jewish learning and tradition, the meaning of a Jewish text.

Words to the Wise

Key terms:

*Ḥumash, Ḥumashim (חוּמָשִׁים)
*Midrash
*Rashi (רַשִׁ"י)
 Rashi script
*Talmud
*Tanach

Other terms:

commentary
folktale
repentance
righteous

Delving into the Chapter

The relationship of fact to legend underlies much of this chapter. Accordingly, after allowing the students sufficient time to read through the chapter (and directing their attention to the time line on pp. 112–13 of the text), you might want to begin discussion by asking them to classify the following statements as fact, falsehood, or legend:

- Rashi's real name was Rabbi Isaac.
- Rashi was born in France.
- Rashi lived before the Talmud was completed.
- Elijah predicted the birth of Rashi.
- Rashi was more precious than any jewel.
- Rashi wrote commentaries on the Torah.
- Rashi made use of Aggadot and Midrashim.
- Rabbi Isaac had a jewel the Emperor wanted.
- Rashi was the father of modern Hebrew.
- Rashi was a wine grower.

You can use this list as a springboard for discussion (have your students write the facts and legends under the correct headings on the chalkboard) or as the basis for a quiz.

Develop your students' sense of the daily rhythm of Rashi's life by assigning the "Rashi's Diary" exercise in the Student Activity Book (p. 69). The next exercise, "Truly Legendary" (p. 70), asks students to write legends based on the lives of real people. After the class has completed the assignment, call on students to read their paragraphs aloud. Whenever a student's story is based on the life of a famous person, have the rest of the class point out the personal qualities (e.g., bravery, beauty, strength, intelligence) revealed in the legend and ask whether the portrait of the famous person in the story matches what students think that person might really be like. The point should be that a legend extends and enriches our understanding of the person and rarely differs radically from prevailing perceptions—perceptions which, in truth, well-established legends helped shape. Legends often express what we don't know but would like to believe about someone.

Up for Discussion

1. Have the class read the Noah story (Genesis 6–9) together with the text paragraphs (pp. 113–14) describing Rashi's commentary on the episode. Have the class answer question (2) in the text (p. 114) by pointing to the exact lines in Genesis. Does the class agree with Rashi's interpretation? Why is it "proper" when speaking with people to give them only some of the praise they deserve, but acceptable, when they are out of earshot, to give them all the praise they deserve? Does the same principle also hold true for blame?

Additional examples of Rashi's exegesis can be found in *Rashi's Commentaries on the Pentateuch*, selected and translated by Chaim Pearl (Norton/B'nai Brith, 1970). See also *Back to the Sources: Reading the Classic Jewish Texts*, edited by Barry W. Holtz (Summit, 1984), for an extended analysis by Rashi of the Hannah story from I Samuel 1.

2. People have different ways of dealing with difficulties in the Torah. Some commentators insist that the plain sense of the text is correct, while others offer naturalistic explanations, claim that the stories are derived from old folktales or ancient documents, or offer new interpretations of what the text "really" means. Introduce to the class the texts in Ḥumash that describe how Eve was created (Genesis 2:18–24), the Tower of Babel (Genesis 11:1–9), the burning bush (Exodus 3:1–6), or the parting of the Red Sea (Exodus 14:21–29), and ask your students how they would interpret these problematic passages.

5. Interpretive techniques are applied not only to stories and books but also to films, popular songs, signs, symbols, and instances of personal behavior.

(**a**) Ask students to "interpret" the following signs:

(b) Have each student say or sing a favorite song lyric and then briefly discuss what the song means.

(c) Ask the class to interpret the following instances of "body language": a clenched fist; two fingers raised in a "V"; two people shaking hands; a right hand placed over one's heart; pointing and shaking a finger at someone. Which gestures are friendly? Hostile? What other emotions or ideas can such gestures express?

Write On!

1. Use the story of "Rashi and the Precious Jewel" (text, pp. 112–13) as the basis for a playlet or paper-bag puppet show to be written and presented by class members.

2. Assign essays of at least two paragraphs based on the following "starters":
- Rashi was a "jewel" because ...
- Rashi proved it's possible to be both a businessman and a scholar by ...
- If Rashi were alive today he would ...
- The same story may be interpreted in many ways because ...
- Legends are an important part of history because ...

3. Tell your students: Write a legend about yourself. You may take on any identity or just be yourself. Explain why you are the "living legend" you claim to be.

4. "Legend for a Day." On separate pieces of paper write the names of important Biblical characters or historical figures mentioned in the text. Fold all the pieces of paper and put them in a bag or box. Have each student pick one piece of paper. The student would then be responsible for doing research on that person and, for an assigned day or period, taking on that character's personality. Dressing up would add further flavor to this activity.

And Finally ...

The "Rashi Box" (Student Activity Book, p. 71) provides a general trivia challenge, while "Take Five" (p. 72) focuses on the material introduced in this chapter.

NOTE: Another reference to Rashi as an interpreter of Ḥumash is found in the text on p. 43.

Answers to "Review It" Questions: p. 114: (1) God wanted Noah to take many years in building the ark so that the wicked would have plenty of time to repent; (2) in the description of Noah as "righteous" while he was listening and "perfectly righteous" when he wasn't.

Answers to Student Activity Book Questions: p. 72: (1) a commentator on the Tanach and Talmud; Rabbi Shlomo Yitzḥaki; (2) his explanation of the Ḥumash; (3) because the Emperor wanted to use the jewel as an eye for his idol; (4) so that the wicked would have plenty of time to ask Noah what he was doing, learn about the coming flood, and repent.

CHAPTER SEVENTEEN

TORAH

Objectives

1. To introduce the concept of Torah in its broadest sense as the totality of Jewish beliefs, practices, and writings.

2. To demonstrate the importance for Jews of teaching Torah to their children.

3. To show that Torah is essential to Jewish life.

Background

The meanings of Torah expand concentrically like ripples on a pond—or, more precisely, given the root meaning of "aiming," like target rings around a bull's-eye. At the center is the Pentateuch, or Five Books of Moses (Ḥumash), contained in the scroll we call the Sefer Torah. But Torah includes more than just the contents of the Sefer Torah. The whole of the Hebrew Bible is also Torah, as are the Halachah and many ideas and practices that are based on the Bible but not found in it. Tanach, Halachah, Aggadah, Midrash, Minhag—these are all forms of Torah, broadly defined, as are the lives of the wise men and women who set examples of righteous behavior.

"Torah" thus includes all Jewish sacred study and, for some moderns, certain secular studies as well. For example, contemporary Hebrew literature is not really "Torah" in the technical sense, but it is so loaded with references to the Jewish religious classics that one must study Torah in order to appreciate the contemporary texts fully. Even the physical sciences can be considered Torah if they lead us more fully to appreciate the intricate beauty of God's creation.

The stories in this chapter reflect the centrality of study within the Jewish tradition. Jews have undergone great trials to preserve their commitment to Jewish learning, and many hero stories testify to how dangerous it can be and has been to study and teach Torah. To what extent do your students and their parents share—or even sympathize with—such commitment and the value system it reflects? How does your class regard those few young Jews who choose to devote their lives to study? And you—do you think of them as "ivory tower types" or as the highest embodiment of Jewish values?

Words to the Wise

Key terms:	Other terms:
*Aggadah	adorned
*Halachah	ancestors
*Ḥumash	cunning
*Ketuvim	descendants
*Minhagim	essential
*Nevi'im	landlord
*Sefer Torah	pledge
*Torah (תּוֹרָה)	

Delving into the Chapter

Read and discuss with the class the introductory definition (text, p. 115), placing special emphasis on the last sentence: "Everything that can teach us how to live properly may be considered Torah." Then ask your students to name (and/or write on the chalkboard) all the Jewish books and ideas that might be considered Torah. Expand the discussion to include Jewish practices and traditions, even the lives of particular men and women, as well as secular studies (if the student can explain how they fit the introductory definition).

After the class has read the entire chapter, challenge your students to explain what the author means when she says: "Torah is more than a way of life. It is a necessity of life." What is a "way of life"? (A profession, being married or not, living in a city or not, moving around a lot or staying put, etc.) What is a "necessity" of life? (Water, air, food, shelter, etc.) In what way is Torah a necessity of *Jewish* life? Could there be any Jewish life without the Sefer Torah? Could Jewish life exist without the Ḥumash? Suppose some dictator ordered the destruction of every Jewish text. Even if Jews could survive such a loss, how would Judaism fare?

One key point to stress is that the true necessities of life are not always recognized. We need air even though we rarely think about our own breathing. Jewish life draws on Torah even when Jews neglect to study it. What makes humans unique among the creatures of the earth is that we can choose to devote ourselves to improving our lives. We can degrade our air and water or we can purify and preserve them. Similarly, as Jews, we can ignore our traditions or even turn away from them, or we can honor and enrich them.

Up for Discussion

1. The introductory definition (text, p. 115) says: "Everything that can teach us how to live properly may be considered Torah." Our parents teach us how to live properly—can they be considered "Torah"? Does your class perceive the relation between a positive answer to this question and the fifth commandment? What other positive influences can students cite in their own lives? (Grandparents, aunts and uncles, favorite teachers, friends, etc.) Can they, too, be considered "Torah"?

2. Most societies require children to attend school. Why is school—or education in general—so important to a society? (To teach skills, inculcate values, create a sense of community, enable the people to make informed choices, ensure society's survival, etc.) What about Jewish schools—how important are they to the survival of the Jewish people?

3. What is a pledge? (Your students will surely make the connection with the "Pledge of Allegiance," but they may not understand the technical meaning of "pledge" as something one person gives to another in order to ensure that a debt will be repaid or a promise fulfilled.) Why did God reject Abraham, Isaac, and Jacob as pledges for the Torah? Why did God rescue the Israelites' pledge of their future leaders and prophets? Which offer did God finally accept? Why are children sometimes called "our nation's most precious resource"? Does your class see any connection between this expression and the pledge story in the chapter?

On the importance of parents and children in the chain of Torah transmission, see p. 76 of the Student Activity Book.

Write On!

1. Rabbi Akiba continued to hold Torah classes even after the Romans declared teaching Torah illegal. Others have also risked pain or punishment in order to hold firm to their beliefs: Nathan Hale ("I only regret that I have but one life to lose for my country"), Patrick Henry ("Give me liberty or give me death!"), Martin Luther King, Jr., Nelson Mandela, Anatoly Shcharansky and the other "refuseniks." Have each student write at least two paragraphs on this assignment: Name at least one belief, ideal, or practice you feel so strongly about that you would be willing to go to prison for it, and explain why it is so important to you.

2. In the text, Rabbi Akiba tells a fable about two animals—a fox and a fish—to explain why the Torah is so important for the Jewish people. Have your students write animal fables of their own to explain the importance to Jews of (a) the Mezuzah, (b) eating Matzah on Passover, (c) fasting on Yom Kippur, or (d) Aseret HaDibrot. Help students who are "stuck" by asking them to consider whether Goldilocks would have entered the home of the three bears if they had put a Mezuzah on their door; to imagine a colony of bees forced suddenly to leave its hive without being able to take with them any honey; or to think of a warren of rabbits that grew weary of living without laws.

And Finally . . .

The Student Activity Book (pp. 73, 77) offers exercises for review and testing.

Answers to "Review It" Questions: p. 120: (1) God found flaws in both the ancestors and the future leaders and prophets of Israel; (2) accepting the children as pledges ensured that the ways of Torah would be transmitted from generation to generation; p. 122: (1) just as a fish cannot live without water, so the Jewish people cannot survive without Torah; (2) the Emperor had made Torah teaching and study a crime punishable by death; the fable portrays abandoning Torah as more dangerous to Jews than continuing to study it.

Answers to Student Activity Book Question: p. 73: All are אֱמֶת except (1) guidance or instruction, (4) children, (5) water, (6) continued; p. 77: (1) Ketuvim, Nevi'im, Halachah, Aggadah, Midrash, etc., when "Torah" is taken in its broadest sense; (3) they were offered to God as pledges by the Israelites; (4) he continued to teach Torah even after the Romans forbade it.

CHAPTER EIGHTEEN

TALMUD

Objectives

1. To describe the Talmud as a collection of Aggadah and Halachah, recording the lives and words of some of the great teachers of the Rabbinic Period.

2. To show how the Gemara amplifies the Mishnah.

Background

The Talmud can be looked at in many ways: as a valuable primary source concerning Jewish life in Roman Palestine and Babylonia, as a reflection of the organic and creative nature of Jewish tradition, and as a document of continuing relevance to Jews who revere tradition and honor Jewish practice. In her "Talmud" chapter, Dr. Pasachoff emphasizes two themes out of the many she might have chosen: first, that two people (or "schools") can disagree or even argue without ceasing to be friends or losing respect for one another; and second, that the Talmud offers evidence not only of the power of tradition but of the process of adaptation.

An extremely valuable essay by Robert Goldenberg in *Back to the Sources* (Summit, 1984) provides a glossary of Talmudic terms, extensive quotations and commentary, and a clear schematic diagram of a sample page of Talmud. Another helpful resource might be Jacob Neusner's *There We Sat Down, or Invitation to the Talmud* (Ktav, 1976). Major themes are discussed in *The Essential Talmud*, by Adin Steinsalz (Bantam, 1976). Each of these authors offers support for the argument that the Talmud represents the adaptive power of Jewish tradition rather than the definitive and unchanging codification of it. If reading the Talmud as evidence for Judaism's adaptive power still seems strange to you, bear in mind that the period of the Mishnah and the Gemara covered more than five centuries, and that the Talmudic era came several hundred years after the official establishment (canonization) of the Bible in Jewish life.

One difficulty in teaching Talmud at this grade level is that the Talmudic text is governed by extremely complicated interpretive (or "hermeneutic") rules and style. Furthermore, some of the rabbinic arguments may seem quite obscure to today's young people—and to their parents, as well. Despite the difficulty of this material, however, it has held sway over traditional Judaism for centuries, and it continues to fascinate young and old alike with its exciting twists and turns. The tight and often minute legal discussions also convey a message about the reverence Jews have for proper observance and for the hallowed ways of determining what proper observance might be.

Without in any way slighting the seriousness of the subject matter, you should try not to overlook the sense of "play" embedded in the Talmudic text. On this subject you might want to examine Samuel Heilman's *People of the Book* (University of Chicago Press, 1983), a personal memoir by a researcher who set out to understand Talmud study groups and himself became an eager and captivated student.

Words to the Wise

Key terms:

*Aggadah

Bet Hillel, Bet Shammai

*Gemara (גְמָרָא)

*Halachah

*Mishnah (מִשְׁנָה)

*Talmud (תַּלְמוּד), Babylonian Talmud, Jerusalem (Palestinian) Talmud

Other terms:

academies

gladiator

humane

mutilation

summarizing

Delving into the Chapter

The opening definition (text, p. 123) establishes a set of pairs—Halachah and Aggadah, Mishnah and Gemara, Jerusalem (Palestinian) and Babylonian Talmuds—that make an appropriate starting point for discussion. If the class has already read the "Aggadah" and "Halachah" chapters (pp. 3–14), you need only review the distinction between narrative and legal materials; you can use the exercise on p. 5 of the Student Activity Book as the basis for an oral quiz that will refresh or sharpen your students' understanding.

For the distinction between Mishnah and Gemara, make sure your students understand that the Mishnah, which is based on oral traditions, is an aggregate of mostly legal material compiled by Yehudah HaNasi in Eretz Yisrael around 200 C.E. During the next three centuries, the Mishnah was itself the subject of commentaries by rabbis in Eretz Yisrael and in Babylonia. The commentaries of the Palestinian rabbis constitute the Palestinian Gemara, which in combination with the Mishnah makes up the Jerusalem or Palestinian Talmud; similarly, the Babylonian Talmud, the larger and more authoritative of the two collections, consists of the Mishnah and the Babylonian Gemara. You'll probably find the chalkboard helpful in clarifying these paired definitions for your students.

Up for Discussion

1. The chapter emphasizes the idea that people can disagree but still remain friends or preserve their mutual respect. For any or all of the following pairs—two classmates, a sister and brother, a parent and a child, the heads of two opposing political parties, the leaders of Israel and Syria, the president of the United States and the general secretary of the Soviet Communist Party—have the class work out five rules that will allow the two sides to disagree without resorting to violence or prolonged hostility. What tactics are fair or unfair? What kinds of putdowns should be avoided? How can the two sides show their respect for each other even while disagreeing?

2. Ask your class: Who do you think was a more effective teacher—Hillel or Shammai? Encourage students to give reasons for their answers.

How might Hillel have applied the answer he gave the non-Jew to the story of Alexander the Great and King Katzya? What criticism might Hillel have made of Alexander's solution to the "gold problem"?

3. The Talmud is an important document for social historians as well as religious thinkers. Ask your students: What does the Talmud tell us about marriage customs in rabbinic times? (See the "Have You Heard" on p. 127 of the text.) What can we learn from the Talmud about ideas of crime and punishment in the ancient world? (See the "Have You Heard" on p. 128.) Imagine the world 2000 years from now. What kinds of things would a historian need in order to have some understanding of what our society was like? What books, movies, magazines, phonograph records, tapes, and television programs might help a future historian get a clear picture of our world today?

Write On!

1. Have your students write their interpretations of the saying "an eye for an eye, a tooth for a tooth." Is this a fair way of paying someone back for an injury? Challenge your students to think of better ways of dispensing punishments and resolving conflicts.

2. Tell your students: Imagine that you are Simeon ben Lakish. Write a brief autobiography, describing what it was like to be poor, your experiences as a gladiator, how you became a scholar, and how you met your wife.

3. Subjects for special reports: Hillel, Simeon ben Lakish, Alexander the Great.

And Finally . . .

Both Duplicating Master #14 and "Take Five" in the Student Activity Book (p. 81) provide a vehicle for review and/or testing.

NOTE: In terms of both vocabulary and content, "Talmud Torah" (text, pp. 131–40) is the obvious successor to the "Torah" and "Talmud" chapters.

Answers to "Review It" Questions: p. 128: (1) (a); (2) when Rabbi Simeon was absent; because their debates were so important to him.

Answers to Student Activity Book Questions: p. 80: 1, 3, and 6 are facts; 2, 4, 5 and 7 are opinions; p. 81: (1) a collection of Halachah and Aggadah *or* a combination of Mishnah and Gemara; (2) Mishnah, Gemara; (3) Jerusalem (or Palestinian), Babylonian; (4) "Don't do to your neighbor anything that you yourself find hateful."

Answers to Duplicating Master #14: Halachah, Aggadah, Mishnah, 200 C.E., Gemara, Jerusalem (or Palestinian), Palestinian (or Jerusalem), Babylonia, Talmud, Babylonian, 500 C.E.

CHAPTER NINETEEN

TALMUD TORAH

Objectives

1. To introduce the concept of Talmud Torah, the Mitzvah of studying and teaching Torah.

2. To show that Jewish learning should be an enjoyable experience.

3. To describe how Rabban Yoḥanan ben Zakkai helped save Judaism by founding a school at Yavneh.

4. To demonstrate that studying Torah should be a lifelong commitment.

Background

"Talmud Torah" represents the happy conjunction of two well-known words to create a new term with a special meaning. Separately each term denotes a body of knowledge or practice; together, the two words signify the act of engaging in Jewish study. "Talmud Torah" appears in most prayer books in the morning service. After a listing of other Mitzvot, we read the expression תַּלְמוּד תּוֹרָה כְּנֶגֶד כֻּלָּם — the study of Torah can be weighed against everything else.

Such phrases arise in a specific context, uttered by a particular person or group of people. We can cite them for various purposes, arguing that practice is more important than study or, conversely, that study is more important than practice. When, as in this case, study is accorded the higher value, we must recognize that we are listening to the claims of scholars. In a contemporary Siddur, *Gates of Prayer*, our modern interpreters have added a flourish: "Study is most important because it leads to practice."

However you as a teacher weigh the relative merits of knowledge and action, there is no question that the study of religious texts is a primary Mitzvah within our tradition. How, then, can you present this imperative to your students in a way that conveys to them some of the power this notion held for so long? One way of approaching the issue is to see how far you can expand the concept of Torah without distorting it. Clearly, the "Torah" in "Talmud Torah" means more than just the Five Books of Moses. Your students' ability to grasp the full meaning of Talmud Torah depends on how well they understand what it means to live a life devoted to studying the Bible, Mishnah, Gemara, and all the commentaries that deal with this literature.

Certainly we can say that the stories extolling the virtues of Talmud Torah — Simon and the honey, Yoḥanan ben Zakkai and Yavneh, Akiba and Rachel — are among the most colorful in the entire volume. They speak of a rich world of legend and drama, even of humor, promising lessons of special vitality for you and your students.

Words to the Wise

Key terms:

*Minhag, Minhagim

Rabban

Sanhedrin (סַנְהֶדְרִין)

Second Temple

*Talmud Torah (תַּלְמוּד תּוֹרָה)

Yavneh

Other terms:

estate

fragrant

humble

ointment

pondered

sacrifices

Delving into the Chapter

An obvious way to lead into this chapter is through a review of the terms "Torah" and "Talmud." The introductory paragraph (text, p. 131) defines "Talmud" as "study," which is perfectly adequate for the present purpose; you might want to make the link between the concept as defined here and the multivolume work discussed in the previous chapter by describing the Talmud itself as the fruits of rabbinic teaching and study of Jewish law and tradition. A review of "Torah" as defined on p. 115 should suffice to broaden the concept of Talmud Torah to include the study of all the Jewish beliefs, practices, and writings that have been handed down through the centuries. As the text on p. 117 makes clear, "Torah" includes not only the Five Books of Moses but the whole of Nevi'im, Ketuvim, Halachah, Aggadah, and Minhagim, as well as the lives of those who embody them. Thus broadened, the concept of Talmud Torah embraces the whole Jewish curriculum.

Your students may already know "Talmud Torah" as another name for a Jewish school. This chapter may thus provide the occasion for some reflection on the contents and purposes of Jewish schooling. What kinds of things have your students learned this year? Do they find their Jewish school experience this year more or less satisfying than that of previous years? What do they have to look forward to as their Bar/Bat Mitzvah and Confirmation years approach? Some students may have switched schools: how does this Jewish school differ from others your students may have known?

This is an excellent time for the rabbi or religious school principal to give a talk on the aims of the Jewish school program and the importance of continuing one's Jewish education. The idea that "you're never too old to study Torah" applies, after all, not just to middle-aged men but to girls and boys who will soon have to choose whether to continue their Jewish schooling beyond Bat or Bar Mitzvah age.

Up for Discussion

1. Let's begin with a review of Yoḥanan ben Zakkai.
    - Who was he? When and where did he live, and what special title did he hold? What problems did the Jews of his time face? Who was the leader of the Roman war against the Jews? Why did Yoḥanan ask the leaders of Jerusalem's Jewish community to surrender to Vespasian? What was their response? Why did Yoḥanan decide to take matters into his own hands? What was his plan for saving Judaism? What did he ask Vespasian to do? What was Vespasian's response? Why do you suppose Vespasian agreed to his request? What happened to the rest of the Jews who remained in Jerusalem? What did the Romans do to the Jerusalem Temple? The Student Activity Book (p. 82) provides a creative way of reviewing this material.

    Now it's time to broaden the questions.
    - The heading in the text (p. 135) reads "How a school for Torah saved Judaism." How does the story of Yoḥanan ben Zakkai bear this out? Rabban Yoḥanan founded a Talmud Torah, which Jews of his time could attend in order to learn about their religious traditions. You, too, attend a Talmud Torah, a school for Judaism. In what ways might today's Jewish schools be said to be "saving" Judaism? How can you help "save" Judaism through your Jewish schooling?

2. This chapter tells us that a person is never too old to start learning Torah. Invite the rabbi or educational director (or the appropriate board member) in to describe your temple's adult study program. Does the temple have an adult Bar/Bat Mitzvah class? Ask the rabbi what opportunities are available for rabbis to continue their own education.

3. Ask your students: How did you feel when you began your Jewish education? Was anything special done on that day? How do you think Jewish schooling might be made "sweeter" for beginning students? How can Jewish education be made more enjoyable for students of any age? "A Sweet Start" is the subject of a Student Activity Book exercise (p. 84).

4. Ask your students: Which do you think is more important—study or doing good deeds? Can you have one without the other? Perhaps students would enjoy formally debating the proposition.

Write On!

1. This chapter offers an abundance of opportunities for special reports:
    (a) Rabban Yoḥanan ben Zakkai;
    (b) Rabbi Akiba;
    (c) Yavneh;
    (d) Sanhedrin;
    (e) Jewish schooling in Roman times or in the ghettos and shtetls of Eastern Europe;
    (f) The American Jewish academies: Hebrew Union College-Jewish Institute of

Religion, Jewish Theological Seminary, Rabbi Isaac Elchanan Theological Seminary of Yeshiva University, Reconstructionist Rabbinical College.

2. Have members of the class interview their grandparents (or elderly aunts and uncles) on what Jewish schooling was like when they were young.

3. Assign compositions (fictional or nonfictional) of at least two paragraphs on the following topics:
- The perfect teacher
- Education can save your life
- A sweet start in school.

4. Stage a debate in which Rabban Yoḥanan ben Zakkai confronts the leaders of Jerusalem on their refusal to surrender to Vespasian. Do the Jews have any real chance of defeating the Roman army? What do the leaders fear will be lost if Jerusalem surrenders? What does Yoḥanan fear will be lost if the Jews continue to hold out?

4. Have students write and perform a dramatic dialogue between Rabban Yoḥanan ben Zakkai and Vespasian. Intensify the drama by having Vespasian, suspicious of Yohanan's motives, question him closely about what he intends to do. More ambitious classes may wish to stage the whole story. Your set designers can create their own versions of the walls and portals of Jerusalem, and several of your more brawny students can attempt to carry the wrapped body of the Rabban through the city gates.

5. Some of your more imaginative students may enjoy rewriting the story of Akiba, Rachel, and the donkey—from the donkey's point of view!

And Finally . . .

Assign "Take Five" (Student Activity Book, p. 85) for review or testing.

NOTE: Only one chapter remains, so be sure to congratulate your students for fulfilling the Mitzvah of Talmud Torah. Duplicating Master #15 provides a form for students to use in creating their own Talmud Torah certificates.

Answers to "Review It" Questions: p. 135: (1) each gets the child off to a good start by presenting study as a rewarding and an enjoyable activity; p. 137: (1) Rabban Yoḥanan left Jerusalem in order to establish an academy at Yavneh; he had to be smuggled out because Jerusalem's leaders would not allow anyone to leave normally; (2) Vespasian knew that Yoḥanan earlier had advocated surrender; he did not realize how important Yoḥanan's request really was; p. 140: (1) from the episode with the donkey Akiba learned that he would only be laughed at for a little while; from seeing how rushing water carved a hole in a granite boulder he saw that if he tried long and hard enough he would be able to learn Torah.

Answers to Student Activity Book Questions: p. 85: (1) literally, "study teaching"; generally, the Mitzvah of studying and teaching Torah; (2) by founding an academy at Yavneh he kept Torah study alive after the destruction of the Second Temple; (3) to give the year a sweet start; (4) dropping a penny on a child's head; spreading honey on the pages of a child's first lesson.

CHAPTER TWENTY

TANACH

Objectives

1. To define Tanach as an acronym that stands for the whole of the Hebrew Bible.
2. To portray the Tanach as a kind of library, offering something to suit every mood.
3. To urge that the study of Tanach never be neglected.

Background

The final chapter offers a relatively brief discussion of the Hebrew Bible. The Hebrew Bible is called "Tanach" by both traditional and modern Jews because the letters of that word represent the Bible's three major sections: Torah, Nevi'im, Ketuvim. You can read more about this term in a book that is probably available in your synagogue library—*The Hebrew Scriptures*, by Samuel Sandmel. (Sandmel uses the spelling "Tanak.")

The Hebrew Bible is often called the Old Testament, but this designation has implications that Jews cannot accept. "Testament" means "covenant": calling the Hebrew scriptures the "Old" Testament and the Christian scriptures the "New" Testament implies that God's "old" covenant with the Jews has been supplanted by a "new" covenant with the Christians. Saying Tanach rather than Old Testament is analogous to our use of B.C.E. and C.E. to avoid the Christological implications of B.C. and A.D. (see p. 12 of the text).

Dr. Pasachoff uses two images to suggest that the Tanach is a vast and wonderful compendium of literature and ideas. The first image, that of the Tanach as a library, is reinforced by the "Tanach Library" exercise on pp. 88–89 of the Student Activity Book. The second image is a more traditional suggestion by a rabbi known as Ben Bag-Bag, a name that should be good for a few giggles. His idea that Bible reading should be a lifelong activity is extremely suggestive. In leafing through the Tanach again and again, in becoming "old and gray in it," we play our part in keeping the Tanach alive.

Words to the Wise

Key terms:

*Ḥumash

*Ketuvim (כְּתוּבִים)

*Leshon HaKodesh

*Nevi'im (נְבִיאִים)

*Tanach (תַּנַ"ךְ)

*Torah (תּוֹרָה)

Other terms:

Aramaic

Ben Bag-Bag

pun

tanaḥ (תַּנַח)

Delving into the Chapter

For most classes this will be a review chapter. "A Tanach Triptych" (Student Activity Book, pp. 86–87) and "In the Tanach Library" (pp. 88–89) are designed as review exercises. Using the Glossary (text, pp. 146–48), you can supplement with defining and spelling "bees" that emphasize the essential vocabulary covered throughout the year.

You might want to pay special heed to puns and acronyms. The Student Activity Book provides "Pun Fun" (p. 90); the climax of this activity should be when students share their puns and illustrations with the rest of the class. Introduce "Tanach" as an acronym for Torah, Nevi'im, and Ketuvim by asking students to identify some well-known abbreviations: e.g., AT&T, FBI, CIA, IBM, UJA, JNF. An acronym like Tanach is a special kind of abbreviation in which the initial letters or groups of letters form a new word: e.g., WAC for Women's Army Corps, SALT for Strategic Arms Limitation Talks, laser for light amplification by stimulated emission of radiation. Kids often enjoy making up names of organizations (silly or serious) to match particular acronyms: you might challenge them with TORAH, JEWS, SEFER, or GELT.

Up for Discussion

1. Speaking of the Tanach, Ben Bag-Bag invites us to "leaf through it and then leaf through it again." Ask students to name their favorite books. Are there any books your students enjoy reading again and again? How does the experience of reading a book for the second or third time differ from that of reading it the first time? Do your students find that as they have grown, a favorite book has taken on new meanings for them?

2. Compare the Tanach with a modern library. Focus on the differences (the modern library is an entire room or building, contains a great many books, has a catalog, etc.) as well as the similarities (each contains a diversity of materials, styles, and literary forms; each is a repository of knowledge and wisdom; each is meant to be sampled rather than read through all at once; etc.). Conduct a lesson in the synagogue library if you have not already done so this year.

Write On!

1. Assign each student to write a story—serious or fanciful—explaining how Ben Bag-Bag got his name. Dramatizations of the stories could be performed with paper-bag puppets.

2. Ben Bag-Bag was a convert to Judaism. Ask each student to write at least two paragraphs giving the reasons why someone might want to convert to Judaism. Encourage your students to make use of some of the basic Jewish ideas and vocabulary they have learned this year.

And Finally . . .

"Take Five" (Student Activity Book, p. 91) and "Tying It All Together" (p. 92) are among the many review activities available to you.

Answers to "Review It" Questions: p. 145: (2) Aggadah, Mishnah, Gemara, Midrash, etc.

Answers to Student Activity Book Questions: pp. 88–89: Items 3, 5, 8, 11, 13, 16, 17, and 19 should be marked T; 1, 4, 7, 10, 14, and 15 should be marked N; and 2, 6, 9, 12, 18, and 20 should be marked K; p. 91: (1) Torah (or Humash)—Creation, early history of the Hebrews, Exodus from Egypt, Aseret HaDibrot and other laws; Nevi'im—the Prophets, the history of the Israelites after their entry into the Promised land; Ketuvim—a collection that includes poems, proverbs, the five Megillot, and other works; (2) the Tanach contains writings to suit any mood; (3) a convert to Judaism who advised Jews to refer often to the Tanach.

MASTER #1
Basic Judaism for Young People
Volume 2: Torah   NAME _____

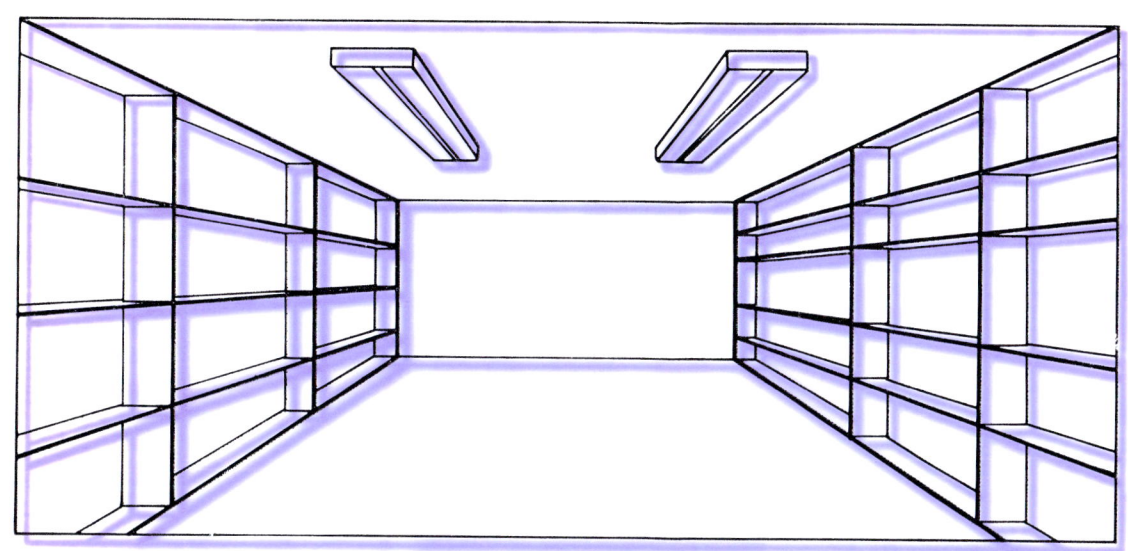

First fill the shelves of this department store with lots of toys, appliances, and other household goods. Make the items as attractive and colorful as possible.

Now imagine that some people have come into your store. Each one sees the scene in a different way; we'll call that way an "interpretation." Read the following interpretations of your scene and match each one with the person most likely to have said it.

1. "If no one buys anything, I'll have to run a big sale tomorrow."

2. "I wish I could afford any of these things."

3. "If Sarah asks me for anything else, I'll tell her we can't afford it."

4. "I think I see someone trying to sneak something out of the store without paying."

5. "Wow, look at that fabulous bike!"

6. "I'd better wait until that guard isn't looking."

7. "Seven hours on my feet—after this next customer, I'm heading home!"

a. Sarah __5__
b. Sarah's mom __3__
c. Thief __6__
d. Store manager __1__
e. Sales clerk __7__
f. Guard __4__
g. A poor person __2__

After you've matched all the people and their "interpretations," you can draw some of these same people—or others of your own choosing—into the scene.

MASTER #1
Basic Judaism for Young People
Volume 2: Torah

NAME _____

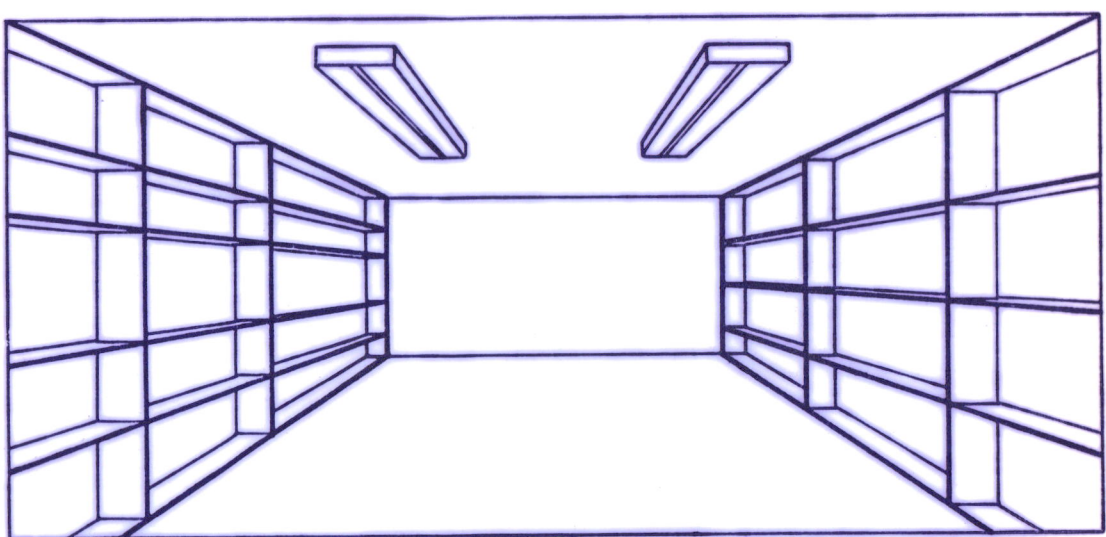

First fill the shelves of this department store with lots of toys, appliances, and other household goods. Make the items as attractive and colorful as possible. Now imagine that some people have come into your store. Each one sees the scene in a different way; we'll call that way an "interpretation." Read the following interpretations of your scene and match each one with the person most likely to have said it.

1. "If no one buys anything, I'll have to run a big sale tomorrow."   a. Sarah _____

2. "I wish I could afford any of these things."   b. Sarah's mom _____

3. "If Sarah asks me for anything else, I'll tell her we can't afford it."   c. Thief _____

d. Store manager _____

4. "I think I see someone trying to sneak something out of the store without paying."   e. Sales clerk _____

5. "Wow, look at that fabulous bike!"   f. Guard _____

6. "I'd better wait until that guard isn't looking."   g. A poor person _____

7. "Seven hours on my feet—after this next customer, I'm heading home!"

After you've matched all the people and their "interpretations," you can draw some of these same people—or others of your own choosing—into the scene.

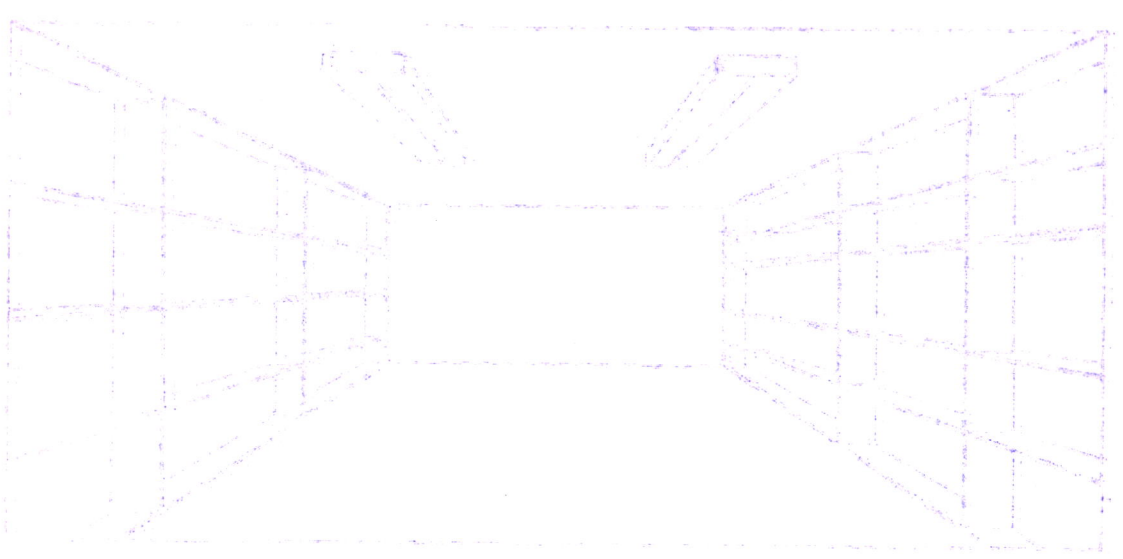

MASTER #1
Basic Judaism for Young People
Volume 2: Torah   NAME _____

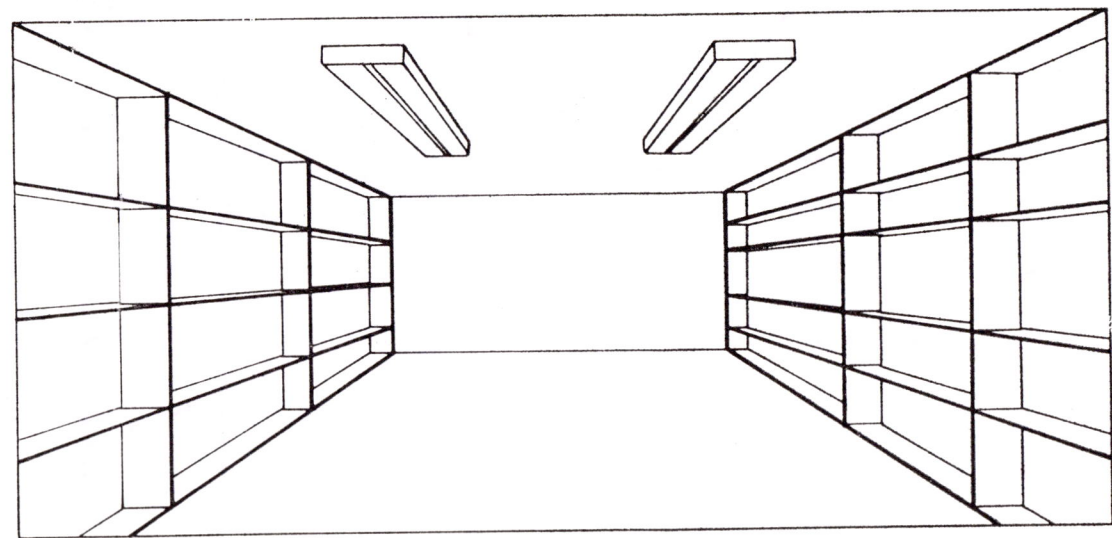

First fill the shelves of this department store with lots of toys, appliances, and other household goods. Make the items as attractive and colorful as possible.

Now imagine that some people have come into your store. Each one sees the scene in a different way; we'll call that way an "interpretation." Read the following interpretations of your scene and match each one with the person most likely to have said it.

1. "If no one buys anything, I'll have to run a big sale tomorrow."

2. "I wish I could afford any of these things."

3. "If Sarah asks me for anything else, I'll tell her we can't afford it."

4. "I think I see someone trying to sneak something out of the store without paying."

5. "Wow, look at that fabulous bike!"

6. "I'd better wait until that guard isn't looking."

7. "Seven hours on my feet—after this next customer, I'm heading home!"

a. Sarah _____
b. Sarah's mom _____
c. Thief _____
d. Store manager _____
e. Sales clerk _____
f. Guard _____
g. A poor person _____

After you've matched all the people and their "interpretations," you can draw some of these same people—or others of your own choosing—into the scene.

MASTER #2
Basic Judaism for Young People
Volume 2: Torah   NAME _____

Fill It Up!

Bible	forty	Rachel	בְּמִדְבַּר	חוּמָשׁ
census	Genesis	Rebecca	בְּרֵאשִׁית	שְׁמוֹת
desert	Leviticus	repetition	דְּבָרִים	
Deuteronomy	Moses	words	וַיִּקְרָא	
Exodus	Numbers	Zipporah		

The first book of the Hebrew __Bible__ is known by the English name __Genesis__. Its Hebrew title is __בְּרֵאשִׁית__, which means "In the beginning." Two famous couples who appear in this book are Isaac and __Rebecca__ and Jacob and __Rachel__.

The second book of the Ḥumash is called __Exodus__, an English word that comes from the Greek for "departure." This book's Hebrew title, __שְׁמוֹת__, means "names." The book includes the story of how Moses and __Zipporah__ met at a well.

Laws for the priests and rituals are given in __Leviticus__, the English name for the third of the five books of the __חוּמָשׁ__. This book's Hebrew title is __וַיִּקְרָא__.

The Hebrew name for the fourth book of the Ḥumash is __בְּמִדְבַּר__, which means "in the desert." In many ways, this title gives a more accurate description of the book's contents than does the English name, __Numbers__. The English title refers to a __census__ conducted in the __desert__.

The fifth of the Five Books of __Moses__ has a long English title, __Deuteronomy__, which means "__repetition__ of the law," and a shorter Hebrew one, __דְּבָרִים__, meaning "__words__." The events in the chapter take place about __forty__ years after the Exodus from Egypt.

MASTER #2
Basic Judaism for Young People
Volume 2: Torah

NAME _____

Fill It Up!

Bible	forty	Rachel	בְּרֵאשִׁית	חֻמָּשׁ
census	Genesis	Rebecca	שְׁמוֹת	שָׁמוֹת
desert	Leviticus	repetition	דְּבָרִים	
Deuteronomy	Moses	words	בַּמִּדְבָּר	
Exodus	Numbers	Zipporah		

The first book of the Hebrew _____ is known by the English name _____. Its Hebrew title is _____, which means "In the beginning." Two famous couples who appear in this book are Isaac and _____ and Jacob and _____.

The second book of the Humash is called _____, an English word that comes from the Greek for "departure." This book's Hebrew title, _____, means "names." The book includes the story of how Moses and _____ met at a well.

Laws for the priests and rituals are given in _____, the English name for the third of the five books of the _____. This book's Hebrew title is _____.

The Hebrew name for the fourth book of the Humash is _____, which means "in the desert." In many ways, this title gives a more accurate description of the book's contents than does the English name, _____. The English title refers to a _____ conducted in the _____.

The fifth of the Five Books of _____ has a long English title, _____, which means "_____ of the law", and a shorter Hebrew one, _____, meaning "_____." The events in the chapter take place about _____ years after the Exodus from Egypt.

MASTER #2
Basic Judaism for Young People
Volume 2: Torah   NAME _____

Fill It Up!

Bible	forty	Rachel	בְּמִדְבַּר	חוּמָשׁ
census	Genesis	Rebecca	בְּרֵאשִׁית	שְׁמוֹת
desert	Leviticus	repetition	דְּבָרִים	
Deuteronomy	Moses	words	וַיִּקְרָא	
Exodus	Numbers	Zipporah		

The first book of the Hebrew _____ is known by the English name _____. Its Hebrew title is _____, which means "In the beginning." Two famous couples who appear in this book are Isaac and _____ and Jacob and _____.

The second book of the Ḥumash is called _____, an English word that comes from the Greek for "departure." This book's Hebrew title, _____, means "names." The book includes the story of how Moses and _____ met at a well.

Laws for the priests and rituals are given in _____, the English name for the third of the five books of the _____. This book's Hebrew title is _____.

The Hebrew name for the fourth book of the Ḥumash is _____, which means "in the desert." In many ways, this title gives a more accurate description of the book's contents than does the English name, _____. The English title refers to a _____ conducted in the _____.

The fifth of the Five Books of _____ has a long English title, _____, which means "_____ of the law," and a shorter Hebrew one, _____, meaning "_____." The events in the chapter take place about _____ years after the Exodus from Egypt.

MASTER #3
Basic Judaism for Young People
Volume 2: Torah

NAME _____

A Ketuvim Crossword

	¹E	Z	R	²A		³P	R	O	⁴V	E	R	⁵B
	S			P		R			O			O
	⁶T	O	P	S		⁷A	N	A	T	I	⁸O	N
	H			A		I			E		⁹M	E
	¹⁰E	C	C	L	E	S	I	¹¹A	S	T	E	S
	R			M		E		V			N	
		¹²L				¹³D		¹⁴J				
	¹⁵L	A	¹⁶M	E	N	T	A	T	I	O	N	¹⁷S
		¹⁸B	O			N		B				O
	¹⁹S	A	R	²⁰A	²¹H			²²M		²³S	O	N
		²⁴N	E	H	E	M	I	A	H			G

ACROSS

1. Priest and scribe
3. A saying
6. Opposite of bottoms
7. Israel is one (two words)
9. ___gillah
10. Takes a serious view of life
15. Sad poems
18. Ruth's husband ___az
19. Rebecca's mother-in-law
23. Jacob's relation to Isaac
24. Leader after the return from exile

DOWN

1. Purim heroine
2. A poem by David (two words)
3. Many prayers _____ God
4. How democracies make decisions
5. Skeleton
8. Sign of the future
11. Tisha b'_____
12. Cheated Jacob
13. Tribe of Israel
14. Good and God-fearing sufferers
16. Opposite of less.
17. _____ of Songs
20. The prophet Jon___
21. Opposite of she
22. What Isaac might have called Sarah

MASTER #3
Basic Judaism for Young People
Volume 2: Torah

NAME _____

A Ketuvim Crossword

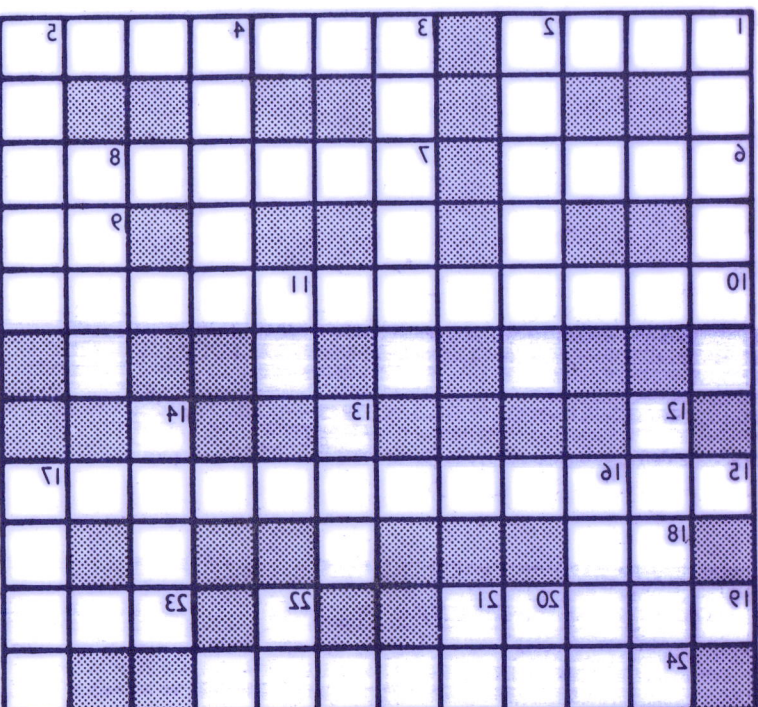

ACROSS

1. Priest and scribe
3. A saying
6. Opposite of bottoms
7. Israel is one (two words)
9. _____ gillah
10. Takes a serious view of life
15. Sad poems
18. Ruth's husband ____az
19. Rebecca's mother-in-law
23. Jacob's relation to Isaac
24. Leader after the return from exile

DOWN

1. Purim heroine
2. A poem by David (two words)
3. Many prayers _____ God
4. How democracies make decisions
5. Skeleton
8. Sign of the future
11. Tisha b'_____
12. Cheated Jacob
13. Tribe of Israel
14. Good and God-fearing sufferers
16. Opposite of less.
17. _____ of songs
20. The prophet Jon____
21. Opposite of she
22. What Isaac might have called Sarah

A Ketuvim Crossword

ACROSS

1.
3.
6.
8.
9.
11.
13.
16.
19.
20.
22.

DOWN

1.
2.
3.
4.
5.
7.
10.
12.
14.
15.
17.
18.
21.
23.

MASTER #3
Basic Judaism for Young People
Volume 2: Torah

NAME _____

A Ketuvim Crossword

ACROSS

1. Priest and scribe
3. A saying
6. Opposite of bottoms
7. Israel is one (two words)
9. ___gillah
10. Takes a serious view of life
15. Sad poems
18. Ruth's husband ___az
19. Rebecca's mother-in-law
23. Jacob's relation to Isaac
24. Leader after the return from exile

DOWN

1. Purim heroine
2. A poem by David (two words)
3. Many prayers _____ God
4. How democracies make decisions
5. Skeleton
8. Sign of the future
11. Tisha b'_____
12. Cheated Jacob
13. Tribe of Israel
14. Good and God-fearing sufferers
16. Opposite of less.
17. _____ of Songs
20. The prophet Jon___
21. Opposite of she
22. What Isaac might have called Sarah

MASTER #4
Basic Judaism for Young People
Volume 2: Torah
NAME _____

Making Ḥumash Count

A number value is given to each letter of the Hebrew alphabet to help us remember important teachings of the Torah. We can also assign number values to all the letters in the English alphabet.

A	B	C	D	E	F	G	H	I	J	K	L	M	N	O	P	Q	R	S	T	U	V	W	X	Y	Z
1	2	3	4	5	6	7	8	9	10	11	12	13	14	15	16	17	18	19	20	21	22	23	24	25	26

For practice, try doing your first name:
LETTERS: _____
NUMBERS: _____ = _____

In the spaces provided, figure out the number value in English of each book of the Ḥumash. Your answer should be a two or three digit number (for example, 23, 168). Put the digit that's farthest to the left in the space labeled "Chapter" and the remaining digits in the space labeled "Verse." (If you have only one digit in the "Verse" column, fine; if you have two, add them together, and write the *sum* of the two digits in the "Verse" column.) Then look in the Bible to find the correct chapter and verse, and copy the verse in the space provided.

Book Title   **Chapter: Verse**   **Write Verse Here**

G E N E S I S

_____   = _7_ : _8_   "Of the clean animals…"

E X O D U S

_____   = _8_ : _8_   "Then Moses and Aaron…"

L E V I T I C U S

_____   = _1_ : _2_   "Speak to the Israelite people…"

N U M B E R S

_____   = _9_ : _2_   "Let the Israelite people…"

D E U T E R O N O M Y

_____   = _1_ : _10_   "The Lord your God has multiplied you…"

MASTER #4
Basic Judaism for Young People
Volume 2: Torah

NAME _____

Making Ḥumash Count

A number value is given to each letter of the Hebrew alphabet to help us remember important teachings of the Torah. We can also assign number values to all the letters in the English alphabet.

A B C D E F G H I J K L M N O P Q R S T U V W X Y Z
1 2 3 4 5 6 7 8 9 10 11 12 13 14 15 16 17 18 19 20 21 22 23 24 25 26

For practice, try doing your first name:

LETTERS: _____
NUMBERS: _____ = _____

In the spaces provided, figure out the number value in English of each book of the Ḥumash. Your answer should be a two or three digit number (for example, 23, 168). Put the digit that's farthest to the left in the space labeled "Chapter," and the remaining digits in the space labeled "Verse." (If you have only one digit in the "Verse" column, fine; if you have two, add them together, and write the sum of the two digits in the "Verse" column.) Then look in the Bible to find the correct chapter and verse, and copy the verse in the space provided.

Book Title	Chapter : Verse	Write Verse Here
G E N E S I S _ _ _ _ _ _ _	___ : ___	_____
E X O D U S _ _ _ _ _ _	___ : ___	_____
L E V I T I C U S _ _ _ _ _ _ _ _ _	___ : ___	_____
N U M B E R S _ _ _ _ _ _ _	___ : ___	_____
D E U T E R O N O M Y _ _ _ _ _ _ _ _ _ _ _	___ : ___	_____

MASTER #4
Basic Judaism for Young People
Volume 2: Torah   NAME _____

Making Ḥumash Count

A number value is given to each letter of the Hebrew alphabet to help us remember important teachings of the Torah. We can also assign number values to all the letters in the English alphabet.

A	B	C	D	E	F	G	H	I	J	K	L	M	N	O	P	Q	R	S	T	U	V	W	X	Y	Z
1	2	3	4	5	6	7	8	9	10	11	12	13	14	15	16	17	18	19	20	21	22	23	24	25	26

For practice, try doing your first name:

LETTERS: _____
NUMBERS: _____ = _____

In the spaces provided, figure out the number value in English of each book of the Ḥumash. Your answer should be a two or three digit number (for example, 23, 168). Put the digit that's farthest to the left in the space labeled "Chapter" and the remaining digits in the space labeled "Verse." (If you have only one digit in the "Verse" column, fine; if you have two, add them together, and write the *sum* of the two digits in the "Verse" column.) Then look in the Bible to find the correct chapter and verse, and copy the verse in the space provided.

Book Title   **Chapter: Verse**   **Write Verse Here**

G E N E S I S

_ _ _ _ _ _ _   = ___ : ___   _____
                                             _____

E X O D U S

_ _ _ _ _ _   = ___ : ___   _____
                                             _____

L E V I T I C U S

_ _ _ _ _ _ _ _ _   = ___ : ___   _____
                                             _____

N U M B E R S

_ _ _ _ _ _ _   = ___ : ___   _____
                                             _____

D E U T E R O N O M Y

_ _ _ _ _ _ _ _ _ _ _   = ___ : ___   _____
                                             _____

MASTER #5
Basic Judaism for Young People
Volume 2: Torah   NAME _____

To solve this puzzle, circle every third English letter, going clockwise from the circled "G." Then insert the English letters in the spaces below. Next, starting with the shin and moving in the opposite direction, circle every third Hebrew letter. Then put the Hebrew letters in the spaces below (we've already marked the vowels below the lines). When you've unlocked the mystery, you should have a good idea of the true meaning of a Mezuzah.

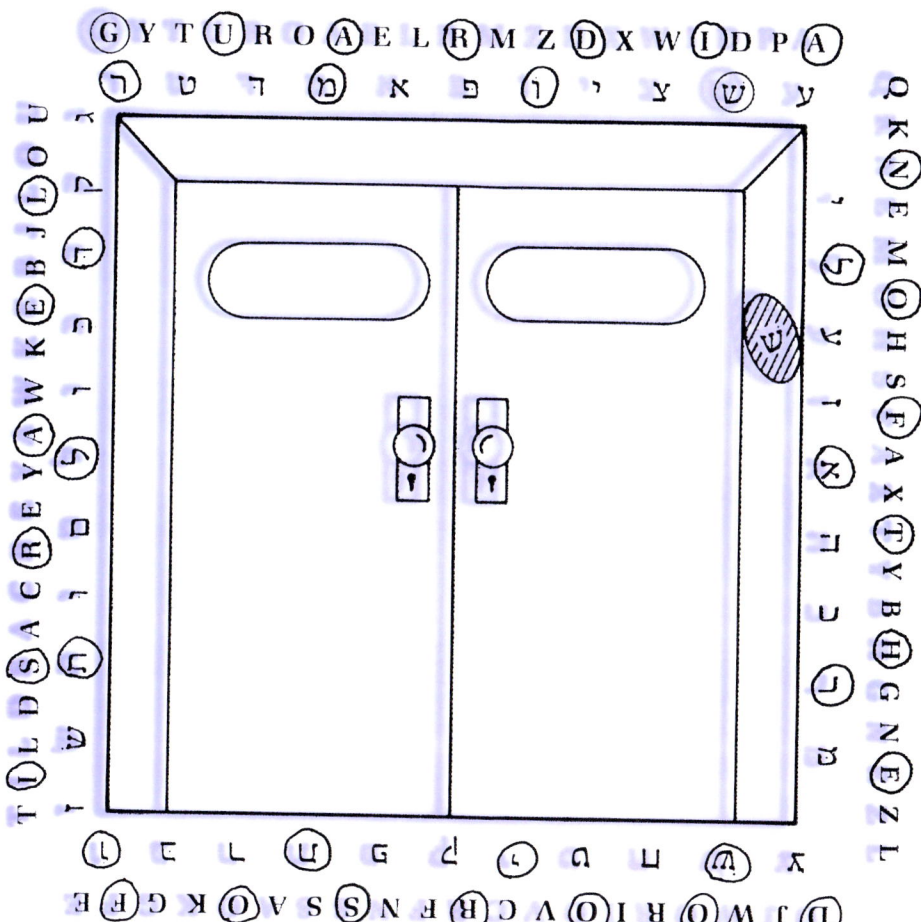

ENGLISH GUARDIAN OF THE DOORS OF ISRAEL

HEBREW שׁוֹמֵר דְּלָתוֹת יִשְׂרָאֵל

MASTER #5
Basic Judaism for Young People
Volume 2: Torah

NAME _____

To solve this puzzle, circle every third English letter, going clockwise from the circled "G." Then insert the English letters in the spaces below. Next, starting with the shin and moving in the opposite direction, circle every third Hebrew letter. Then put the Hebrew letters in the spaces below (we've already marked the vowels below the lines). When you've unlocked the mystery, you should have a good idea of the true meaning of a Mezuzah.

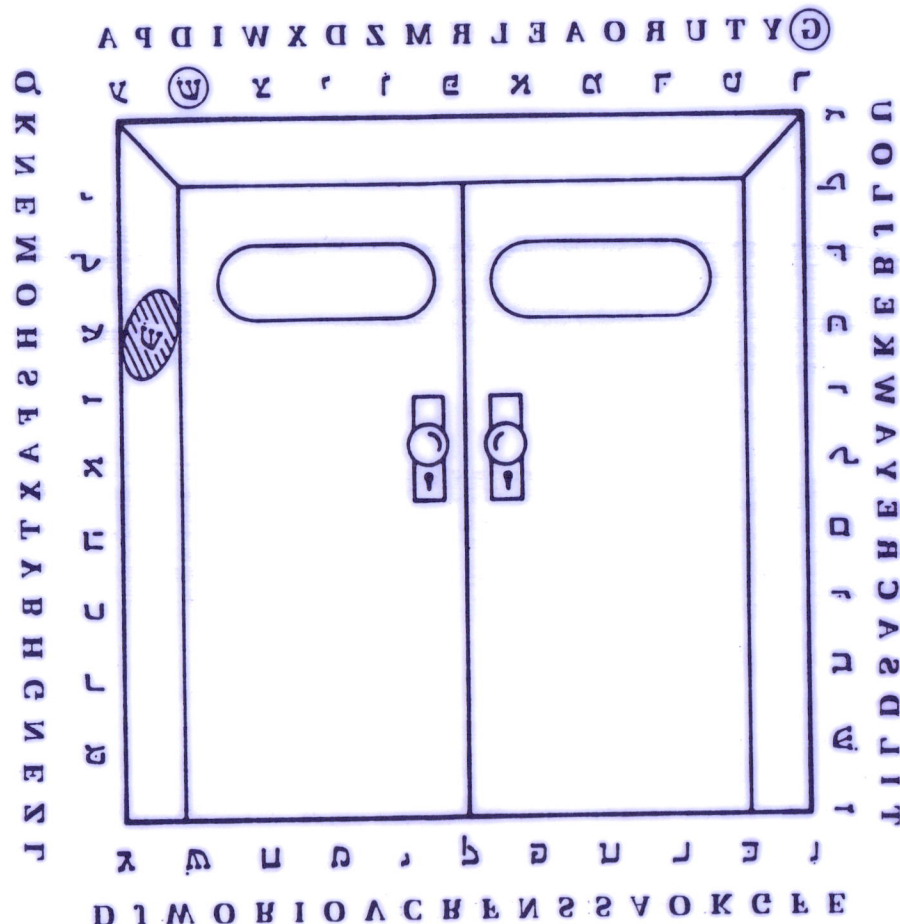

ENGLISH _ _ _ _ _ _ _   _ _   _ _ _

HEBREW _ _ _ _ _ _

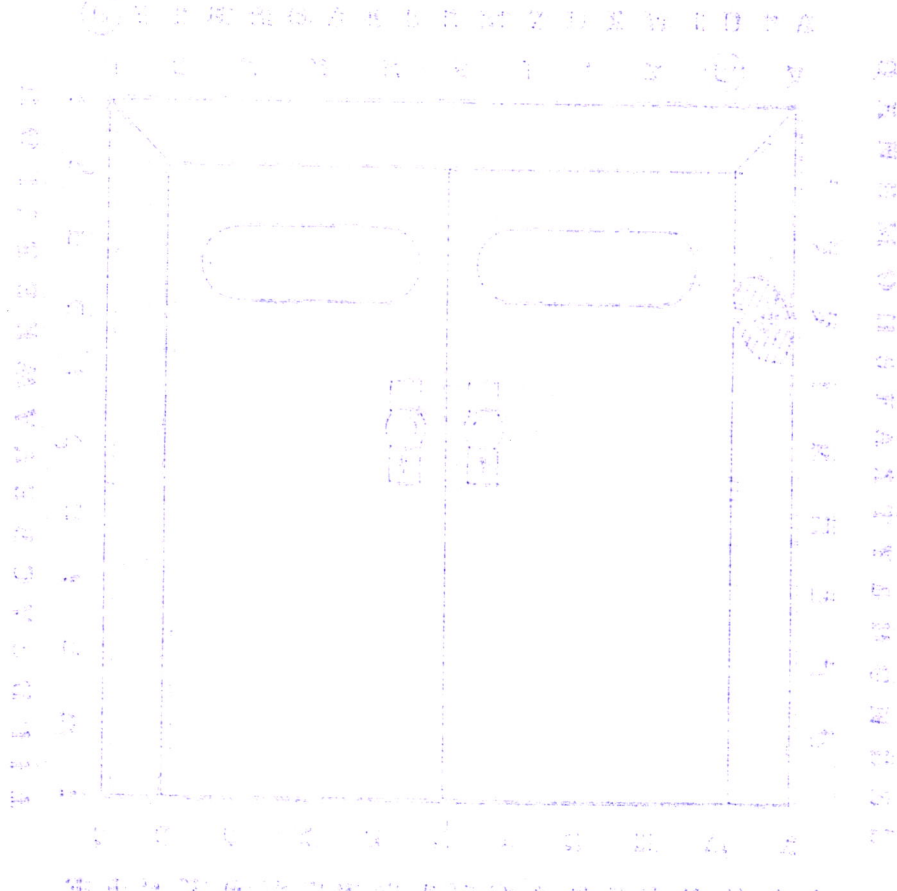

MASTER #5
Basic Judaism for Young People
Volume 2: Torah   NAME _____

To solve this puzzle, circle every third English letter, going clockwise from the circled "G." Then insert the English letters in the spaces below. Next, starting with the shin and moving in the opposite direction, circle every third Hebrew letter. Then put the Hebrew letters in the spaces below (we've already marked the vowels below the lines). When you've unlocked the mystery, you should have a good idea of the true meaning of a Mezuzah.

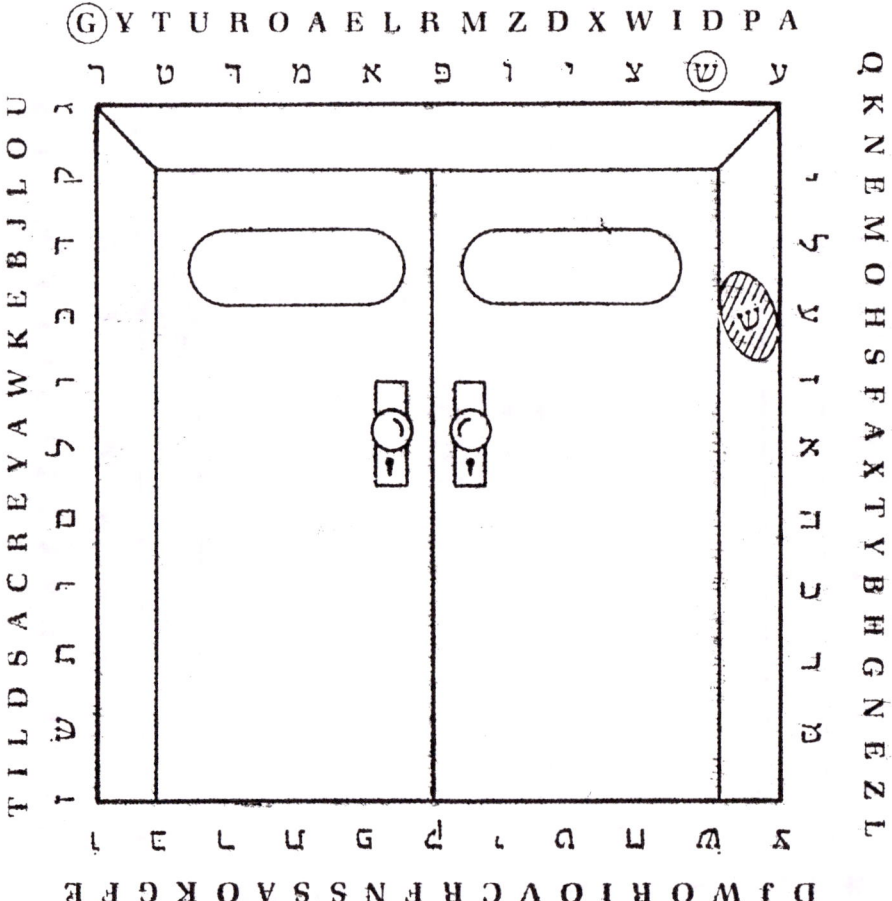

ENGLISH _____ _____ _____ _____ _____ _____ _____

HEBREW _____ _____ _____ _____ _____ _____

MASTER #6
Basic Judaism for Young People
Volume 2: Torah   NAME _____

HANUKKAH PAINTBRUSH COOKIES

Mix thoroughly:

⅓ cup soft shortening

⅓ cup sugar

1 egg

⅔ cup honey

1 teaspoon vanilla

Stir in:

2¾ cups sifted flour

1 teaspoon baking soda

1 teaspoon salt

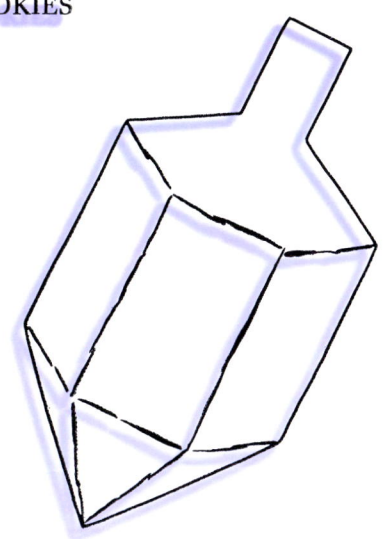

Roll dough into a ball and refrigerate until chilled (about 30 minutes). Heat oven to 350°F. While oven is heating, roll out the chilled dough on a floured board, using a flour-covered rolling pin. Roll to ¼" thickness. Using metal molds, cut in different shapes (menorahs, dreidels, coins, etc.). Place shapes on greased cookie sheet. Paint designs with *egg yolk paint* (see below). Bake 8–10 minutes. To keep colors clear, do not let cookies brown. Yield: five dozen 2½" cookies.

Egg yolk paint. Blend well 1 egg yolk and ¼ teaspoon water. Divide mixture among several small dishes or cups. To each dish add a drop of a different food color. Paint colored designs on cookies with small, clean brushes.

Try these Ḥanukkah Paintbrush Cookies in class or at home. Maybe they'll become part of your family's Ḥanukkah Minhagim!

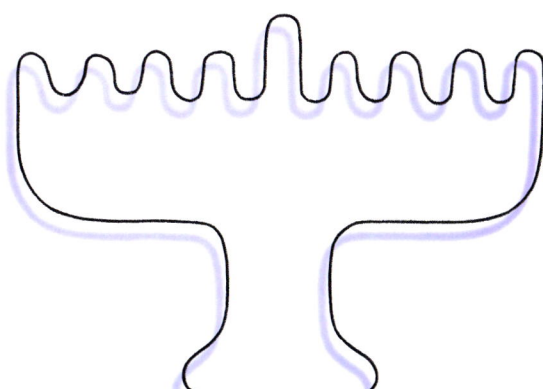

MASTER #6
Basic Judaism for Young People
Volume 2: Torah

NAME _____

HANUKKAH PAINTBRUSH COOKIES

Mix thoroughly:
⅓ cup soft shortening
⅓ cup sugar
1 egg
¼ cup honey
1 teaspoon vanilla

Stir in:
2¾ cups sifted flour
1 teaspoon baking soda
1 teaspoon salt

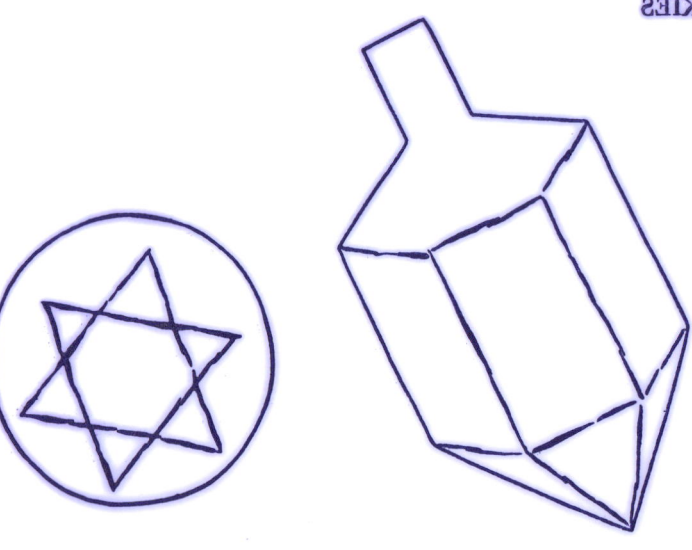

Roll dough into a ball and refrigerate until chilled (about 30 minutes). Heat oven to 350°F. While oven is heating, roll out the chilled dough on a floured board, using a flour-covered rolling pin. Roll to ¼" thickness. Using metal molds, cut in different shapes (menorahs, dreidels, coins, etc.). Place shapes on greased cookie sheet. Paint designs with egg yolk paint (see below). Bake 8 – 10 minutes. **To keep colors clear, do not let cookies brown.** Yield: five dozen 2½" cookies.

Egg yolk paint. Blend well 1 egg yolk and ¼ teaspoon water. Divide mixture among several small dishes or cups. To each dish add a drop of a different food color. Paint colored designs on cookies with small, clean brushes.

Try these Hanukkah Paintbrush Cookies in class or at home. Maybe they'll become part of your family's Hanukkah Minhagim!

MASTER #6
Basic Judaism for Young People
Volume 2: Torah   NAME _____

HANUKKAH PAINTBRUSH COOKIES

Mix thoroughly:

1/3 cup soft shortening

1/3 cup sugar

1 egg

2/3 cup honey

1 teaspoon vanilla

Stir in:

2 3/4 cups sifted flour

1 teaspoon baking soda

1 teaspoon salt

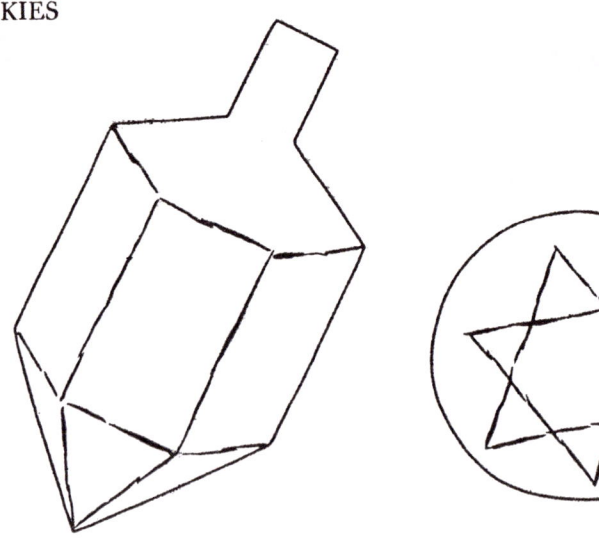

Roll dough into a ball and refrigerate until chilled (about 30 minutes). Heat oven to 350°F. While oven is heating, roll out the chilled dough on a floured board, using a flour-covered rolling pin. Roll to 1/4" thickness. Using metal molds, cut in different shapes (menorahs, dreidels, coins, etc.). Place shapes on greased cookie sheet. Paint designs with *egg yolk paint* (see below). Bake 8–10 minutes. To keep colors clear, do not let cookies brown. Yield: five dozen 2 1/2" cookies.

Egg yolk paint. Blend well 1 egg yolk and 1/4 teaspoon water. Divide mixture among several small dishes or cups. To each dish add a drop of a different food color. Paint colored designs on cookies with small, clean brushes.

Try these Hanukkah Paintbrush Cookies in class or at home. Maybe they'll become part of your family's Hanukkah Minhagim!

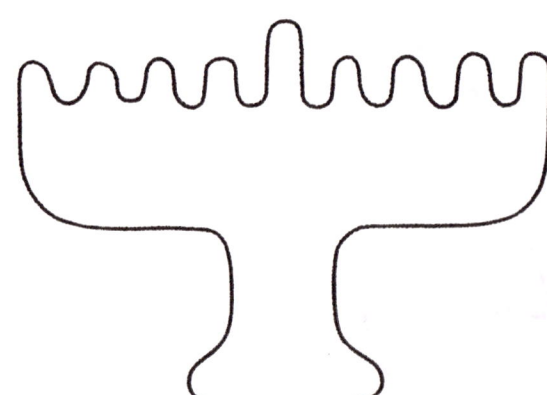

MASTER #7
Basic Judaism for Young People
Volume 2: Torah   NAME _____

Cut out these Ḥanukkah coins.
Arrange them in the style of a crossword puzzle so you can spell the words
MINHAG, HALACHAH, CUSTOM, MITZVAH, and LAW.

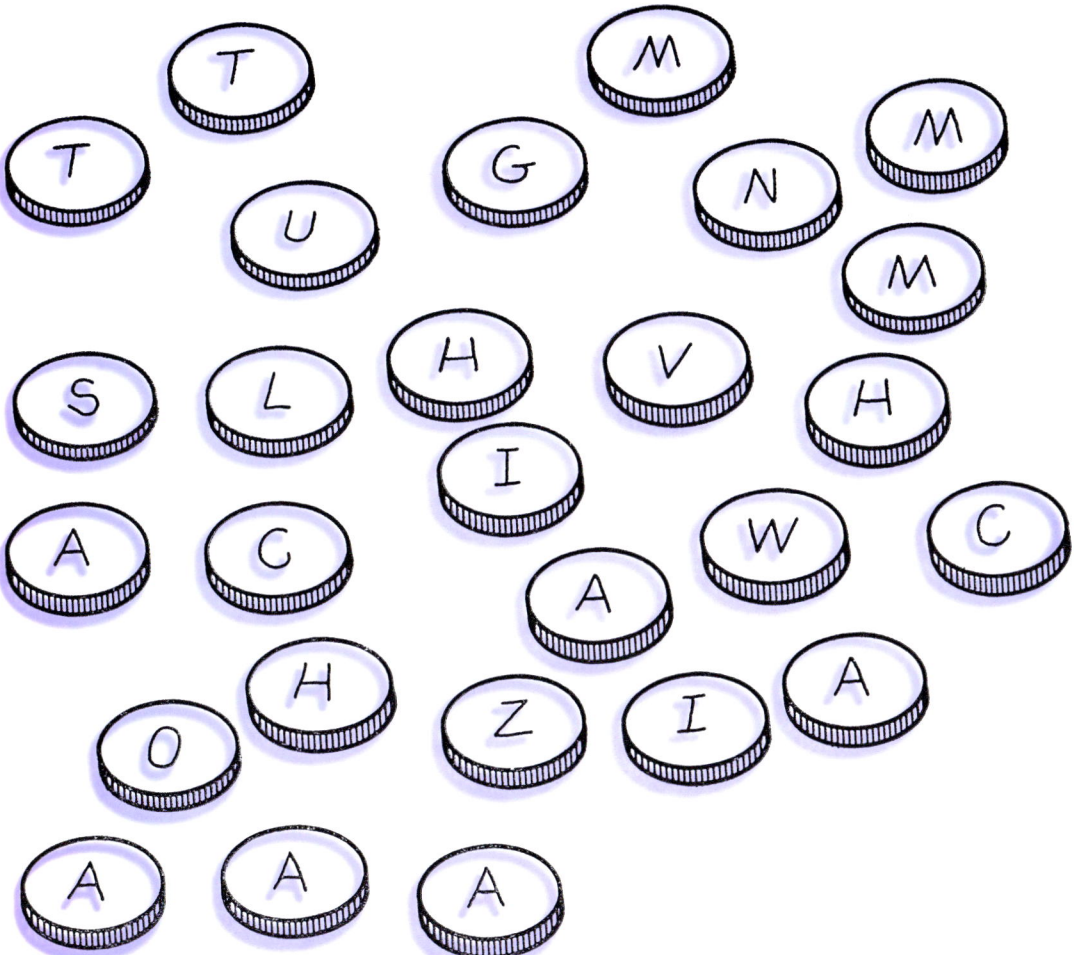

MASTER #7:
Basic Judaism for Young People
Volume 2: Torah

NAME _____

Cut out these Ḥanukkah coins.
Arrange them in the style of a crossword puzzle so you can spell the words MINHAG, HALACHAH, CUSTOM, MITZVAH, and LAW.

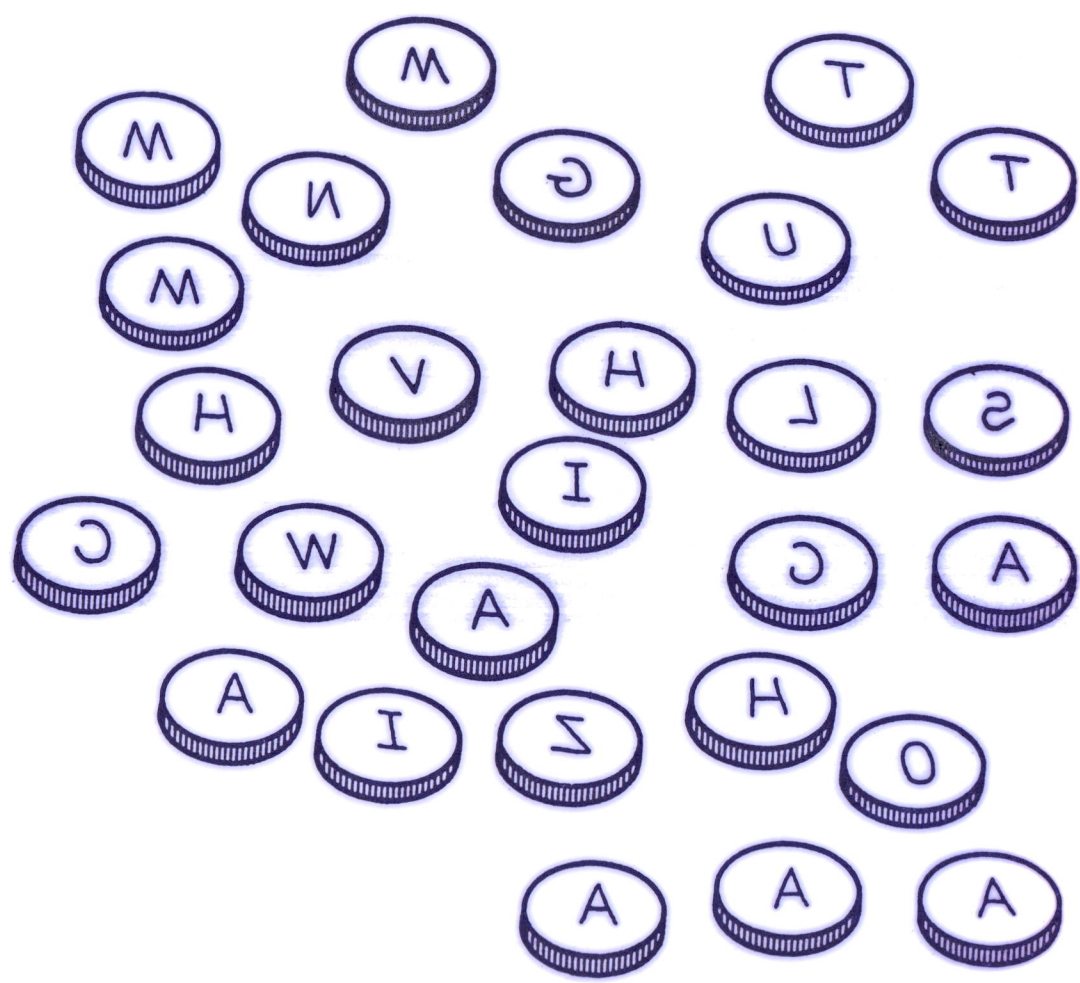

Judaism for Young People
Volume 2: Torah   NAME _____

Cut out these Hanukkah coins.
Arrange them in the style of a crossword puzzle so you can spell the words
MINHAG, HALACHAH, CUSTOM, MITZVAH, and LAW.

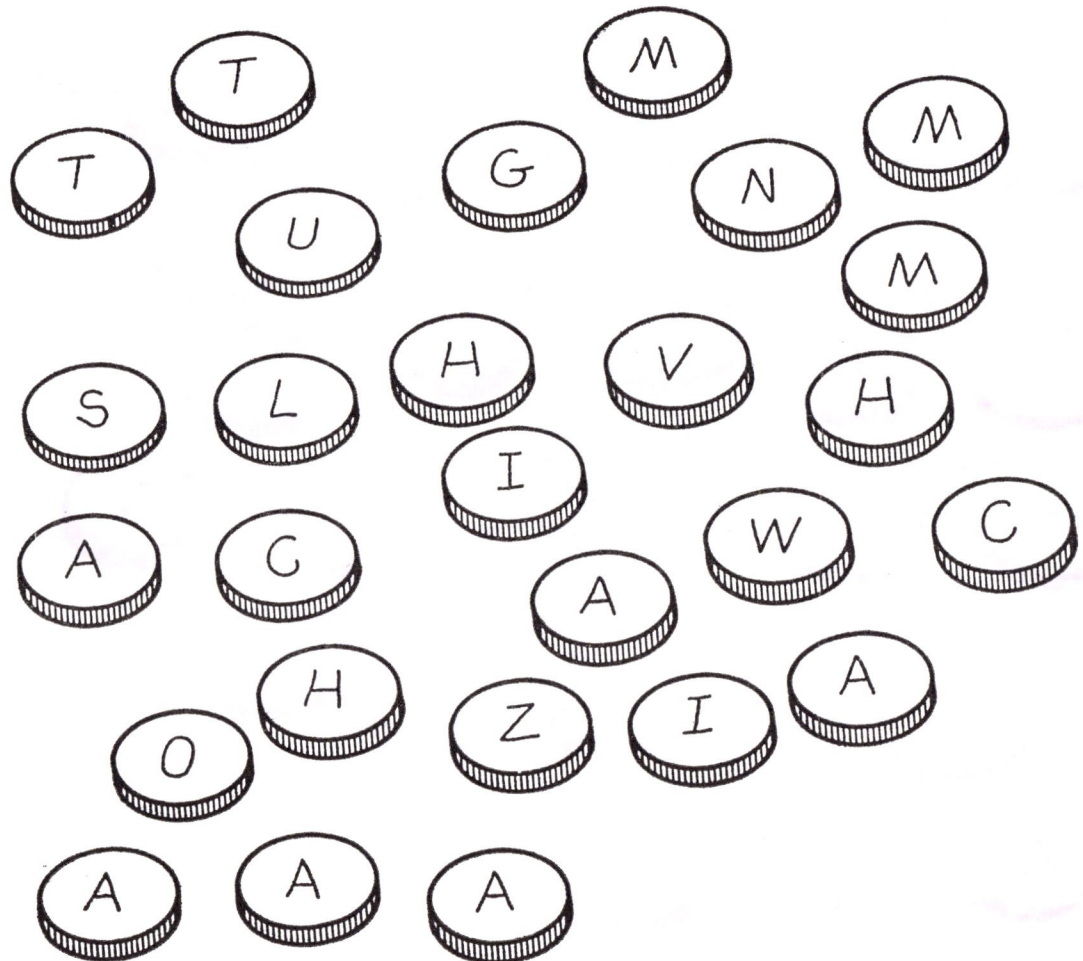

MASTER #8
Basic Judaism for Young People
Volume 2: Torah

NAME _____

Ḥumash, Nevi'im, Ketuvim

The Hebrew Bible, or Tanach, consists of three sections: Ḥumash (חוּמָשׁ), Nevi'im (נְבִיאִים), and Ketuvim (כְּתוּבִים). Label each of the following books ח, נ, or כ, depending on which section of the Tanach it belongs to. If the book does *not* belong to the Tanach, leave the space blank.

1. Psalms __כ__
2. Exodus __ח__
3. Lamentations __כ__
4. Joshua __נ__
5. Proverbs __כ__
6. Isaiah __נ__
7. Kings __נ__
8. Genesis __ח__
9. Haggadah _____
10. Ruth __כ__

11. Deuteronomy __ח__
12. Ecclesiastes __כ__
13. Jonah __נ__
14. Midrash _____
15. Ezra __כ__
16. Leviticus __ח__
17. Gemara _____
18. Jeremiah __נ__
19. Esther __כ__
20. Samuel __נ__

MASTER #8
Basic Judaism for Young People
Volume 2: Torah

NAME _____

Humash, Nevi'im, Ketuvim

The Hebrew Bible, or Tanach, consists of three sections: Humash (חומש), Nevi'im (נביאים), and Ketuvim (כתובים). Label each of the following books ח, נ, or כ, depending on which section of the Tanach it belongs to. If the book does not belong to the Tanach, leave the space blank.

1. Psalms _____   11. Deuteronomy _____
2. Exodus _____   12. Ecclesiastes _____
3. Lamentations _____   13. Jonah _____
4. Joshua _____   14. Midrash _____
5. Proverbs _____   15. Ezra _____
6. Isaiah _____   16. Leviticus _____
7. Kings _____   17. Gemara _____
8. Genesis _____   18. Jeremiah _____
9. Haggadah _____   19. Esther _____
10. Ruth _____   20. Samuel _____

REVIEW #6
Bible Judaism for Young People
Volume 2: Tanak   NAME_____

Humash, Nevi'im, Ketuvim

The Hebrew Bible or Tanakh consists of three sections: Humash (חומש), Nevi'im (נביאים), and Ketuvim (כתובים). Label each of the following books H, N, or K depending on which section of the Tanakh it belongs to. If the book does not belong to the Tanakh, leave the space blank.

1. Esther _____   11. Deuteronomy _____
2. Exodus _____   12. Ecclesiastes _____
3. Lamentations _____   13. Jonah _____
4. Joshua _____   14. Leviticus _____
5. Proverbs _____   15. Ezra _____
6. Isaiah _____   16. Judith _____
7. Kings _____   17. Genesis _____
8. Genesis _____   18. Jeremiah _____
9. Haggadah _____   19. Esther _____
10. Ruth _____   20. Samuel _____

MASTER #8
Basic Judaism for Young People
Volume 2: Torah   NAME _____

Ḥumash, Nevi'im, Ketuvim

The Hebrew Bible, or Tanach, consists of three sections: Ḥumash (חוּמָשׁ), Nevi'im (נְבִיאִים), and Ketuvim (כְּתוּבִים). Label each of the following books ח, נ, or כ, depending on which section of the Tanach it belongs to. If the book does *not* belong to the Tanach, leave the space blank.

1. Psalms _____
2. Exodus _____
3. Lamentations _____
4. Joshua _____
5. Proverbs _____
6. Isaiah _____
7. Kings _____
8. Genesis _____
9. Haggadah _____
10. Ruth _____

11. Deuteronomy _____
12. Ecclesiastes _____
13. Jonah _____
14. Midrash _____
15. Ezra _____
16. Leviticus _____
17. Gemara _____
18. Jeremiah _____
19. Esther _____
20. Samuel _____

MASTER #9
Basic Judaism for Young People
Volume 2: Torah

NAME _____

Cause and Effect

Many of the Nevi'im saw a clear connection between the bad things people do and the punishments they receive, and between the good things people do and the rewards they get. Complete your personal cause-and-effect chart by filling in the blanks below:

CAUSE	EFFECT
If I don't do my homework	Then I will _____
If I fasten my car seat belt	Then I won't _____
If I volunteer to do extra chores	Then I can _____
If I talk back to my parents	Then they will _____
If I never smoke cigarettes	Then I will _____
If I'm always late for school	Then I won't _____
If I forget to take out the garbage	Then I may _____
If I study Torah	Then I will _____

MASTER #9
Basic Judaism for Young People
Volume 2: Torah

NAME _____

Cause and Effect

Many of the Nevi'im saw a clear connection between the bad things people do and the punishments they receive, and between the good things people do and the rewards they get. Complete your personal cause-and-effect chart by filling in the blanks below:

CAUSE	EFFECT
If I don't do my homework	Then I will _____
If I fasten my car seat belt	Then I won't _____
If I volunteer to do extra chores	Then I can _____
If I talk back to my parents	Then they will _____
If I never smoke cigarettes	Then I will _____
If I'm always late for school	Then I won't _____
If I forget to take out the garbage	Then I may _____
If I study Torah	Then I will _____

MASTER #9
Basic Judaism for Young People
Volume 2: Torah   NAME_____

Cause and Effect

Many of the God laws are about consequences between the bad things people do and the punishment they receive, and between the good things people do and the reward they get. Complete your own cause-and-effect chart by filling in the blanks below:

CAUSE   EFFECT

If I don't do my homework   Then I will _____
                                      _____

If I fasten my car seat belt   Then I won't _____
                                      _____

If I volunteer to do extra chores   Then I can _____
                                      _____

If I talk back to my parents   Then they will _____
                                      _____

If I never smoke cigarettes   Then I will _____
                                      _____

If I'm always late for school   Then I won't _____
                                      _____

If I forget to take out the garbage   Then I may _____
                                      _____

If I study Torah   Then I will _____
                                      _____

MASTER #9
Basic Judaism for Young People
Volume 2: Torah   NAME _____

Cause and Effect

Many of the Nevi'im saw a clear connection between the bad things people do and the punishments they receive, and between the good things people do and the rewards they get. Complete your personal cause-and-effect chart by filling in the blanks below:

CAUSE	EFFECT
If I don't do my homework	Then I will _____
If I fasten my car seat belt	Then I won't _____
If I volunteer to do extra chores	Then I can _____
If I talk back to my parents	Then they will _____
If I never smoke cigarettes	Then I will _____
If I'm always late for school	Then I won't _____
If I forget to take out the garbage	Then I may _____
If I study Torah	Then I will _____

MASTER #10
Basic Judaism for Young People
Volume 2: Torah   NAME _____

Adorning the Sefer Torah

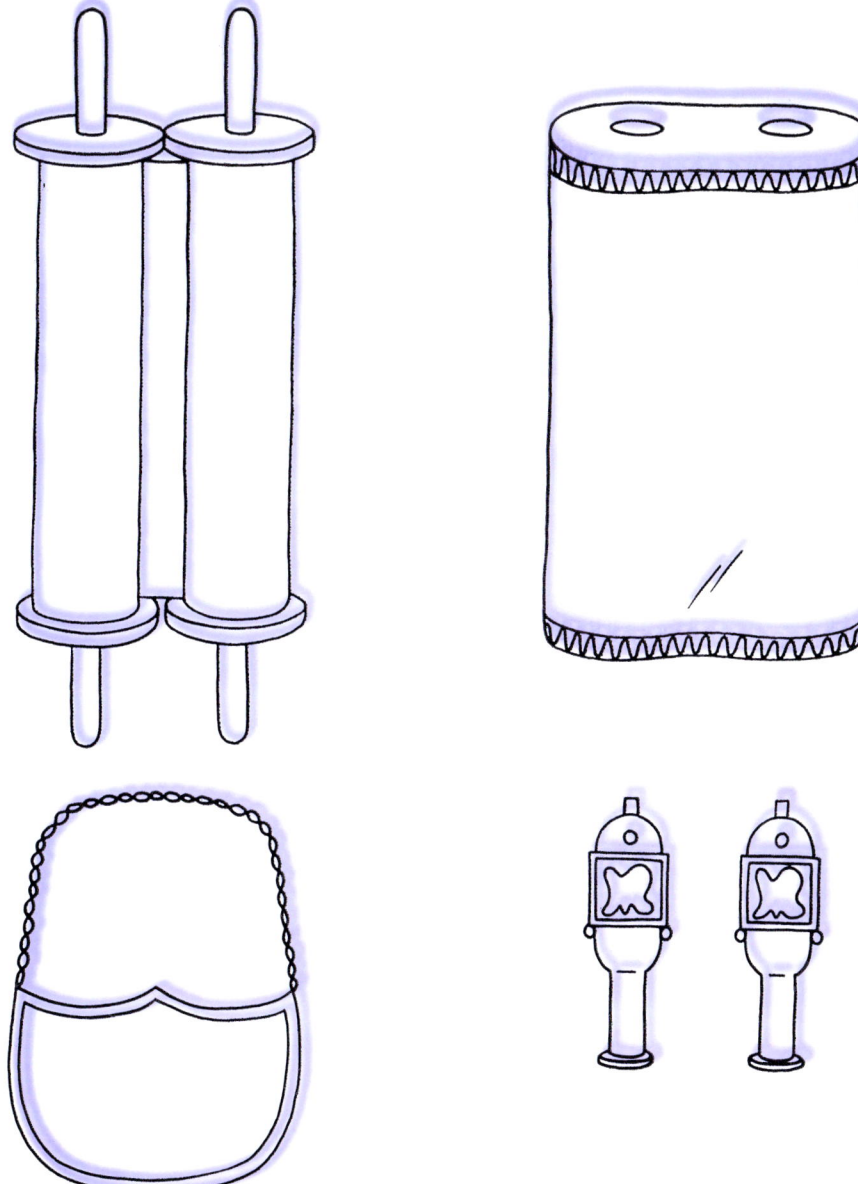

One way of showing love for the Sefer Torah is by decorating it as beautifully as we can. Using crayons or colored pens, make the mantle, breastplate, and crowns as fancy as you want. Then cut out the separate parts and use glue to assemble your own Sefer Torah.

MASTER #10
Basic Judaism for Young People
Volume 2: Torah

NAME _____

Adorning the Sefer Torah

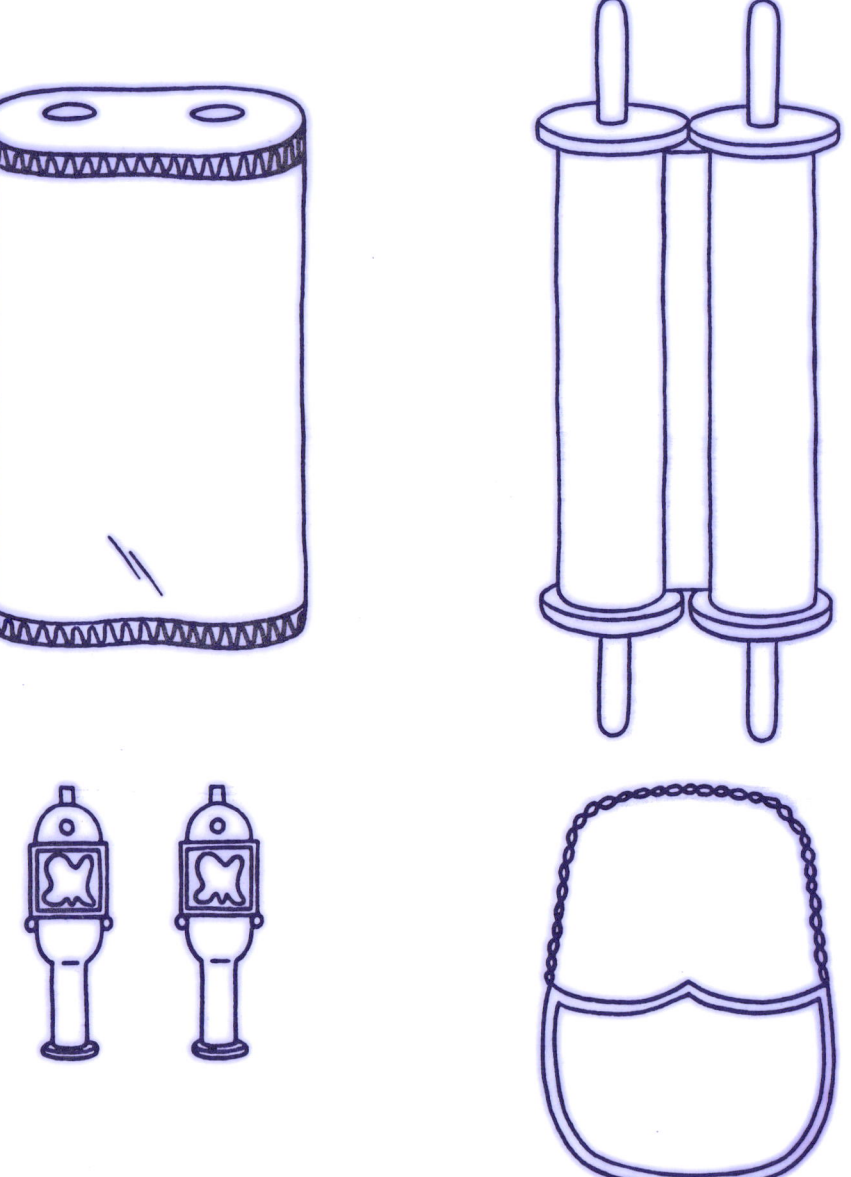

One way of showing love for the Sefer Torah is by decorating it as beautifully as we can. Using crayons or colored pens, make the mantle, breastplate, and crowns as fancy as you want. Then cut out the separate parts and use glue to assemble your own Sefer Torah.

MASTER #10
Basic Judaism for Young People
Volume 2: Torah

NAME _____

Adorning the Sefer Torah

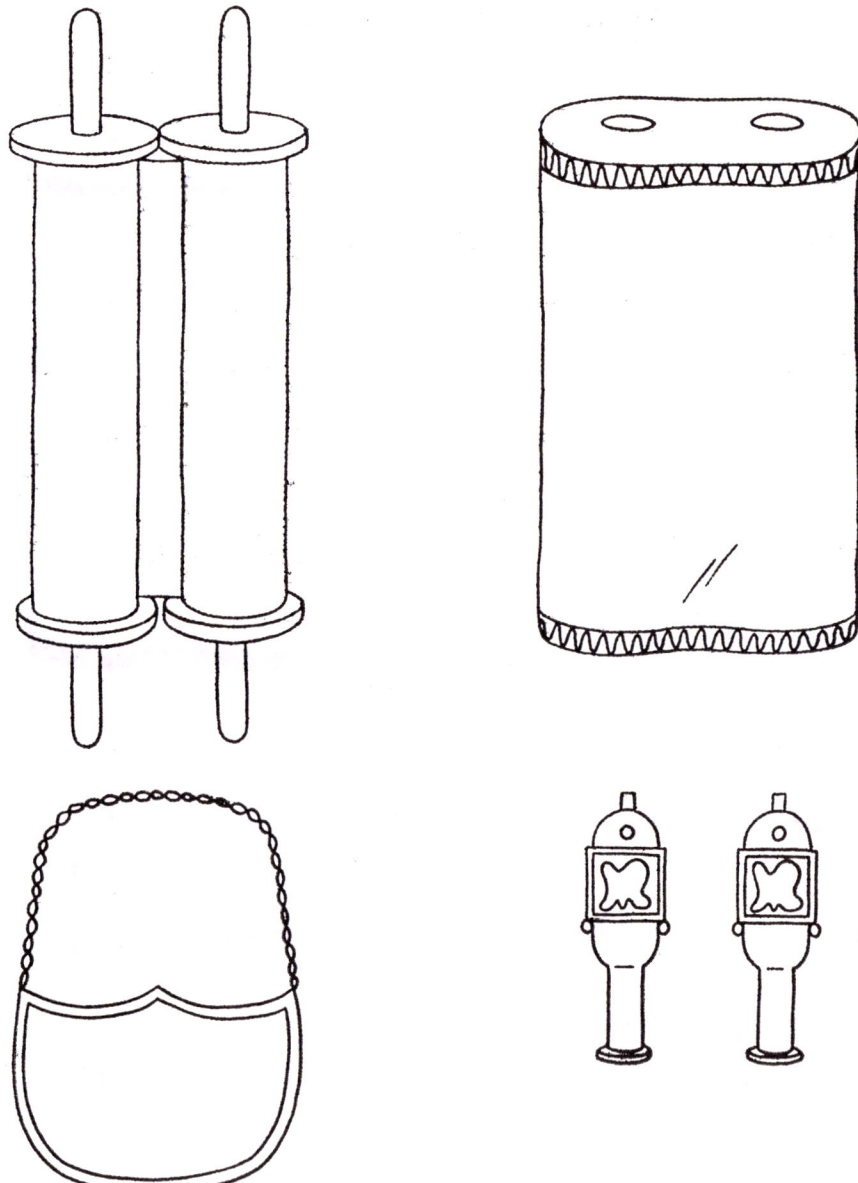

One way of showing love for the Sefer Torah is by decorating it as beautifully as we can. Using crayons or colored pens, make the mantle, breastplate, and crowns as fancy as you want. Then cut out the separate parts and use glue to assemble your own Sefer Torah.

MASTER #11
Basic Judaism for Young People
Volume 2: Torah   NAME _____

Cut out these letters and paste them in the correct order to spell out four occasions on which a person can receive an Aliyah. Paste them on a separate sheet of paper and illustrate each event.

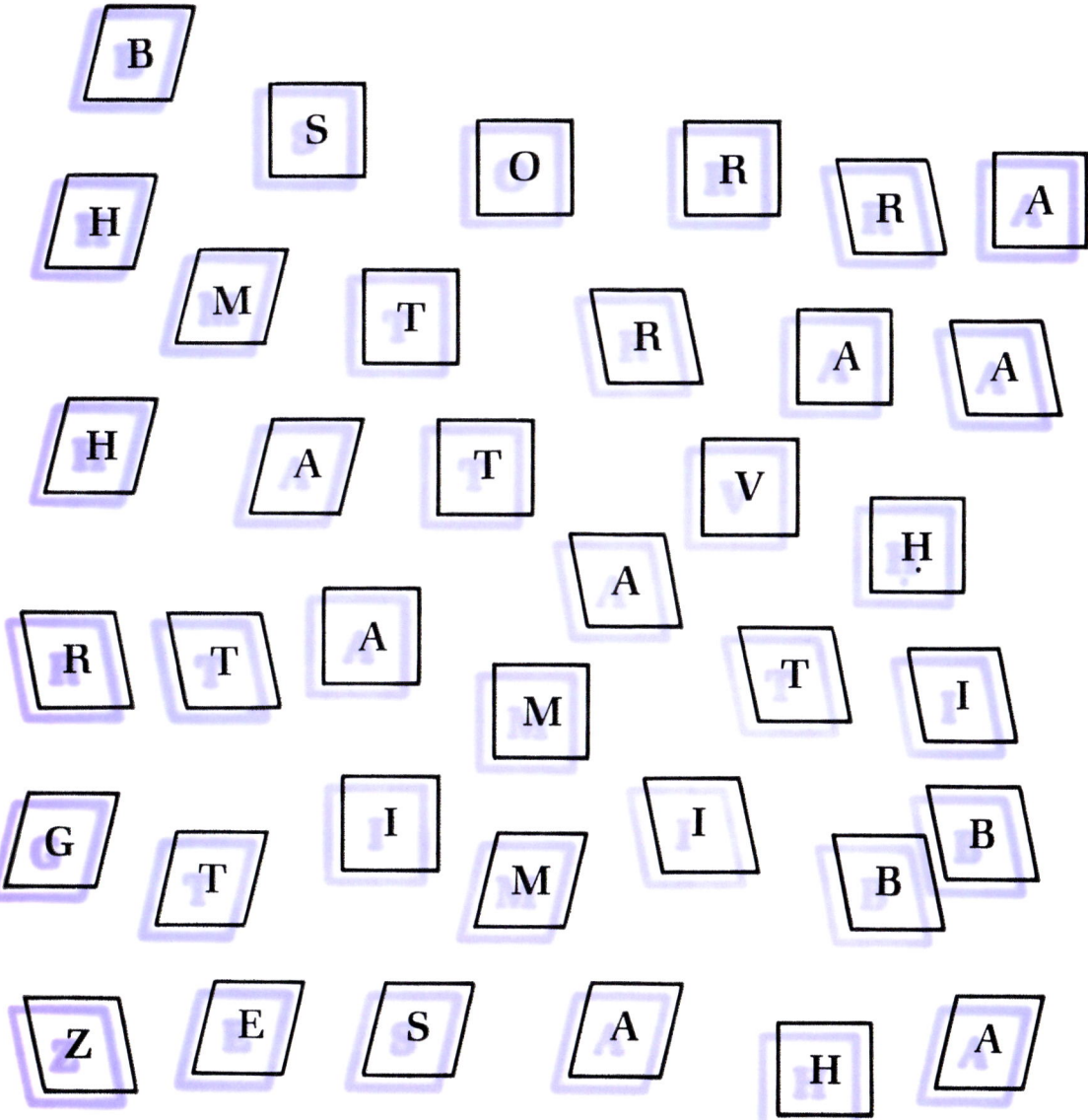

MASTER #11
Basic Judaism for Young People
Volume 2: Torah

NAME _____

Cut out these letters and paste them in the correct order to spell out four occasions on which a person can receive an Aliyah. Paste them on a separate sheet of paper and illustrate each event.

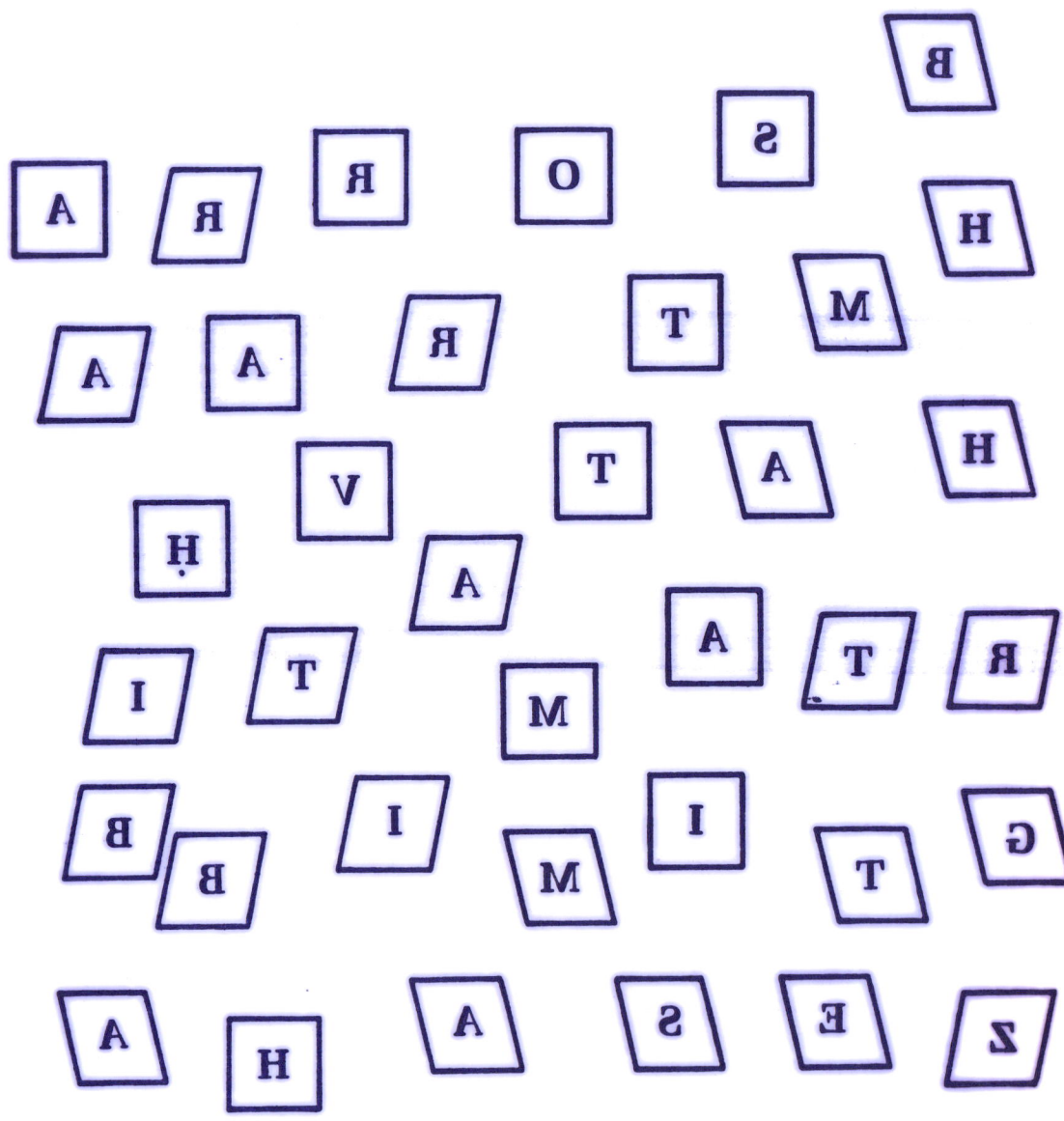

MASTER #11
Basic Judaism for Young People
Volume 2: Torah   NAME _____

Cut out these letters and paste them in the correct order to spell out four occasions on which a person can receive an Aliyah. Paste them on a separate sheet of paper and illustrate each event.

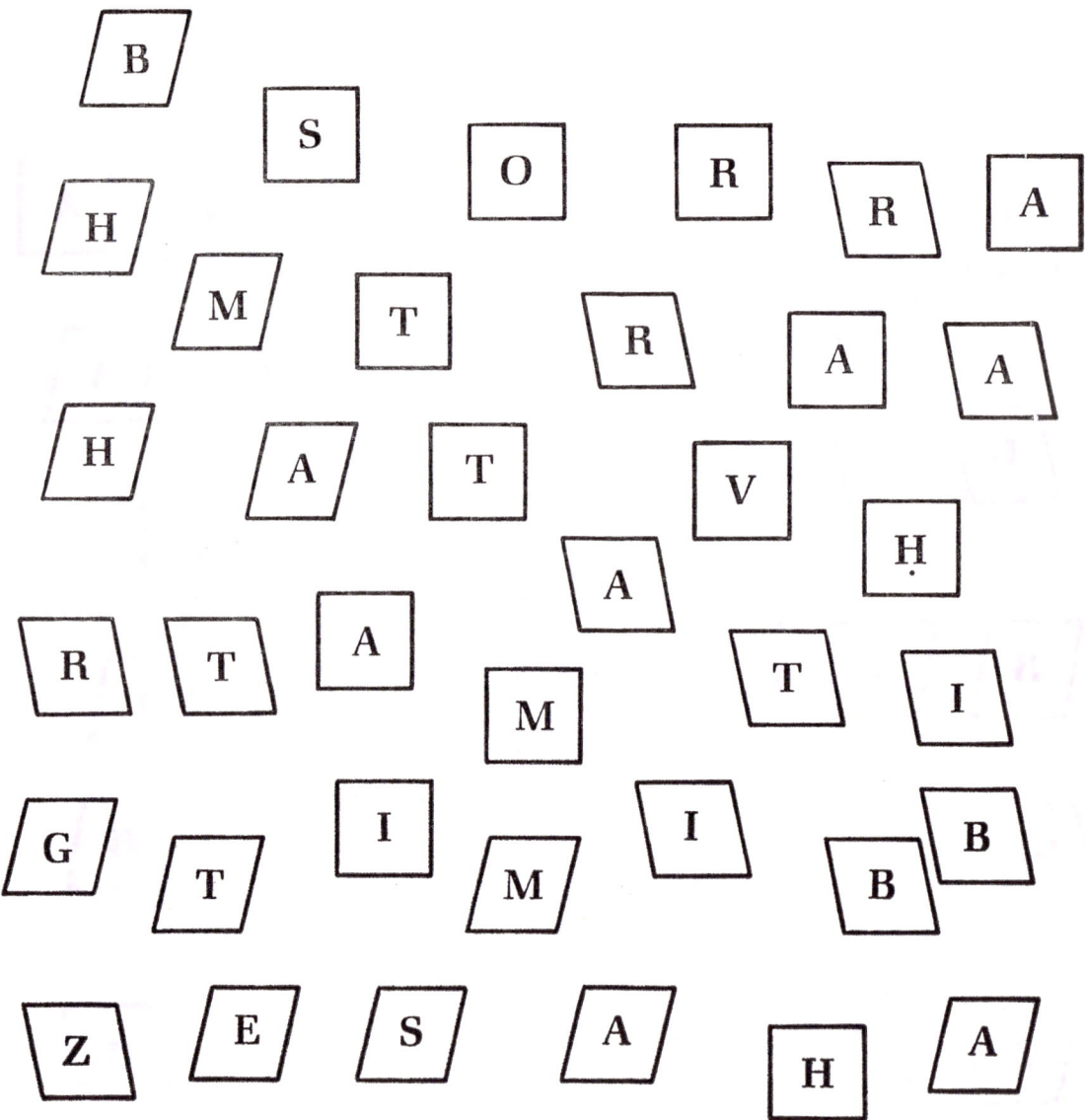

MASTER #12
Basic Judaism for Young People
Volume 2: Torah

NAME _____

On each of the spokes of the wheel below, write an important stage in a person's life. Starting with birth, continue clockwise with such important events as going to school, getting married, or having children, and end with death. In the space next to each event, draw a picture of a Jewish practice, custom, or ceremony connected with it.

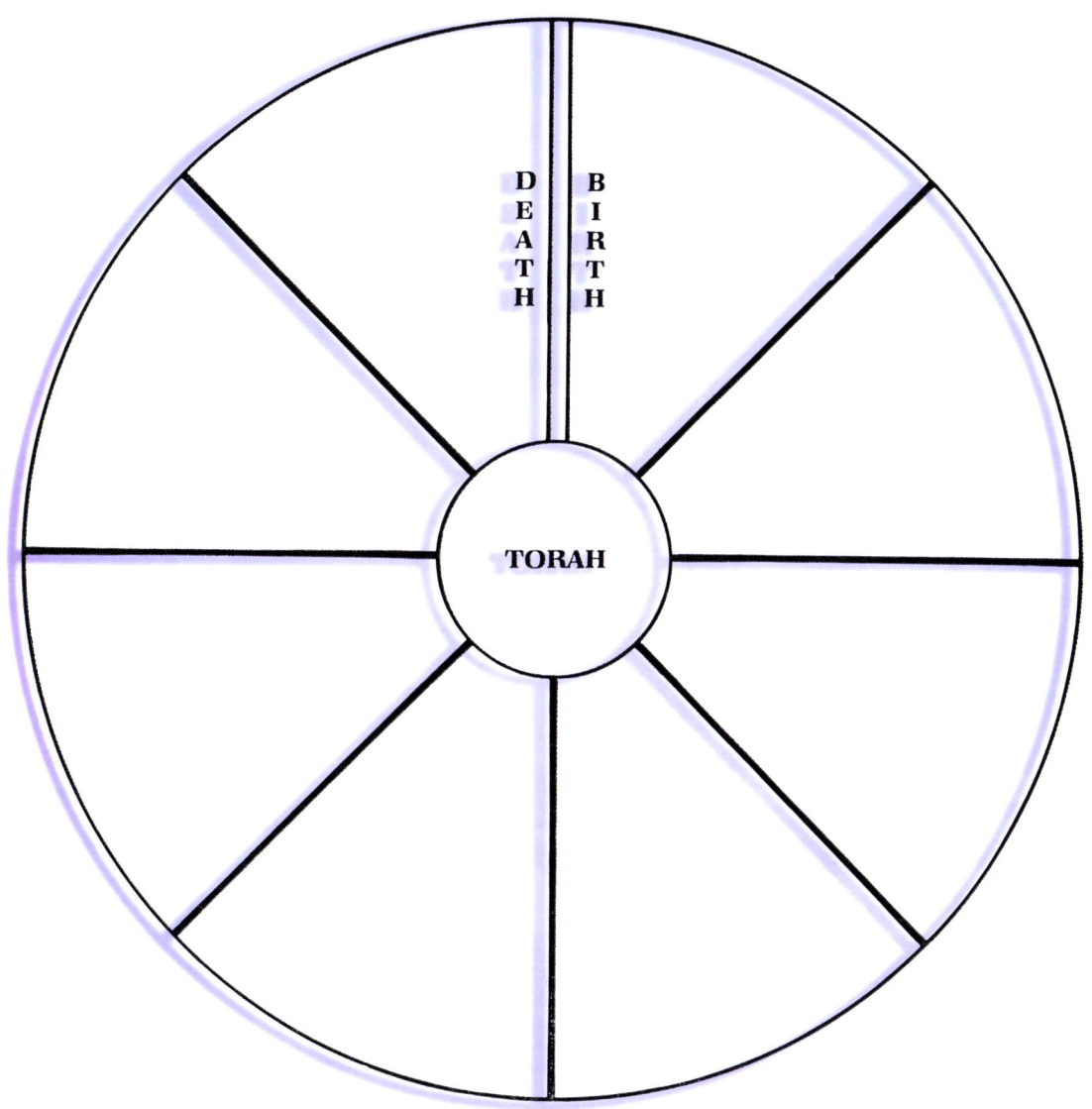

MASTER #12
Basic Judaism for Young People
Volume 2: Torah

NAME _____

On each of the spokes of the wheel below, write an important stage in a person's life. Starting with birth, continue clockwise with such important events as going to school, getting married, or having children, and end with death. In the space next to each event, draw a picture of a Jewish practice, custom, or ceremony connected with it.

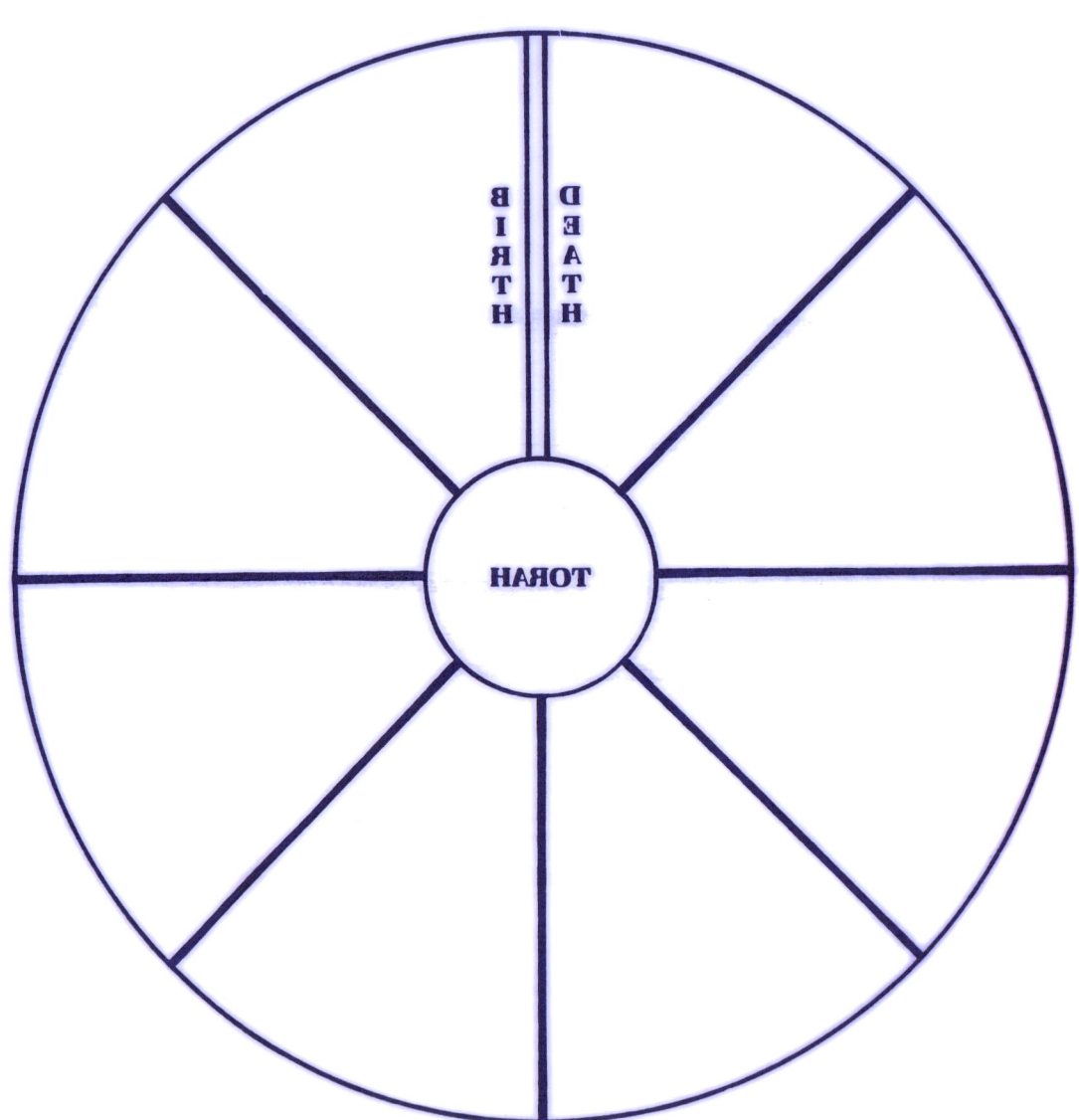

MASTER #12
Basic Judaism for Young People
Volume 2: Torah   NAME _____

At each of the spokes of the wheel below, write an important stage in a person's life. Starting with birth, continue clockwise with such important events as going to school, getting married, or having children, and end with death. In the space next to each event, draw a picture of a Jewish practice, custom, or ceremony associated with it.

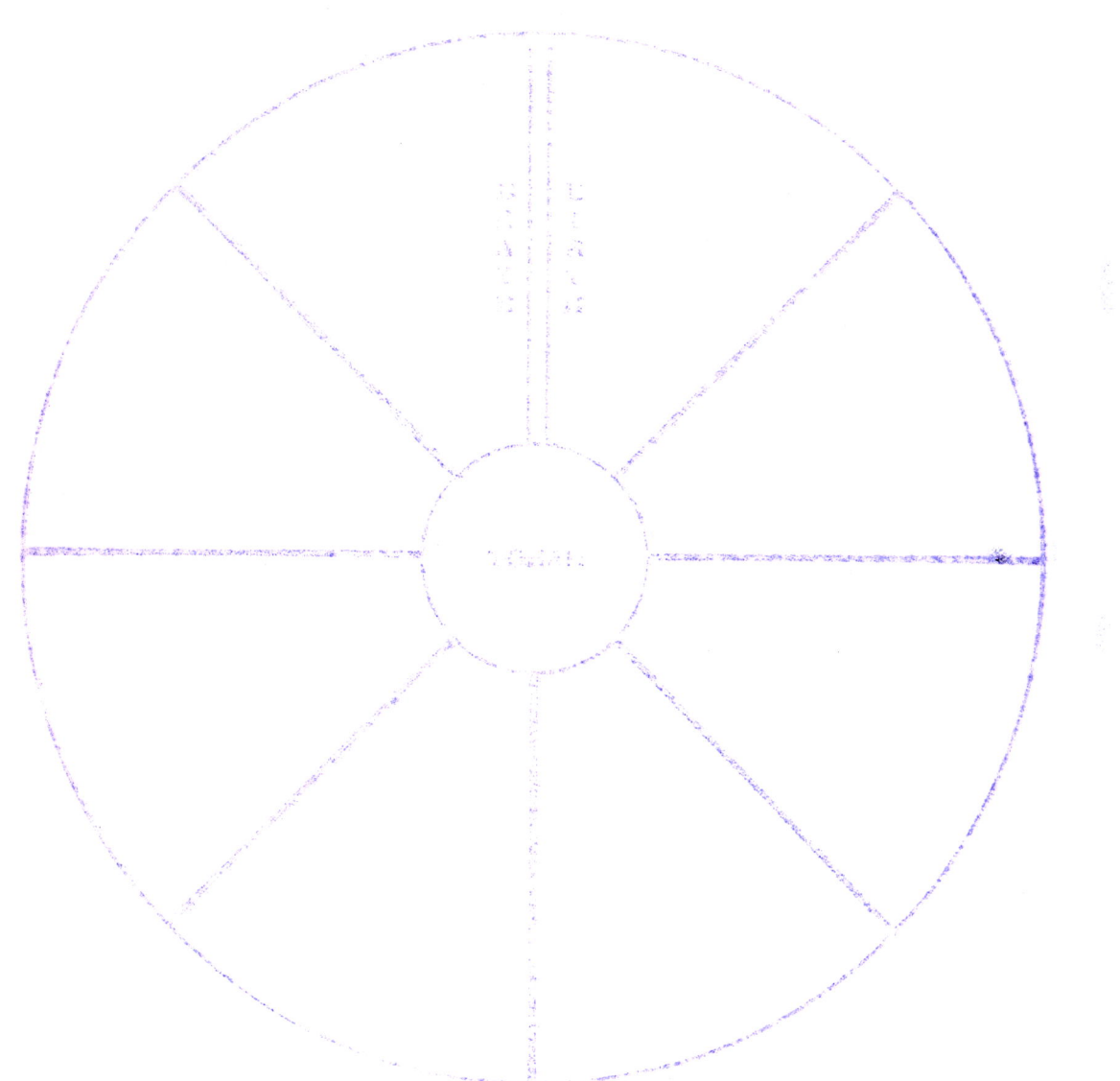

MASTER #12
Basic Judaism for Young People
Volume 2: Torah

NAME _____

On each of the spokes of the wheel below, write an important stage in a person's life. Starting with birth, continue clockwise with such important events as going to school, getting married, or having children, and end with death. In the space next to each event, draw a picture of a Jewish practice, custom, or ceremony connected with it.

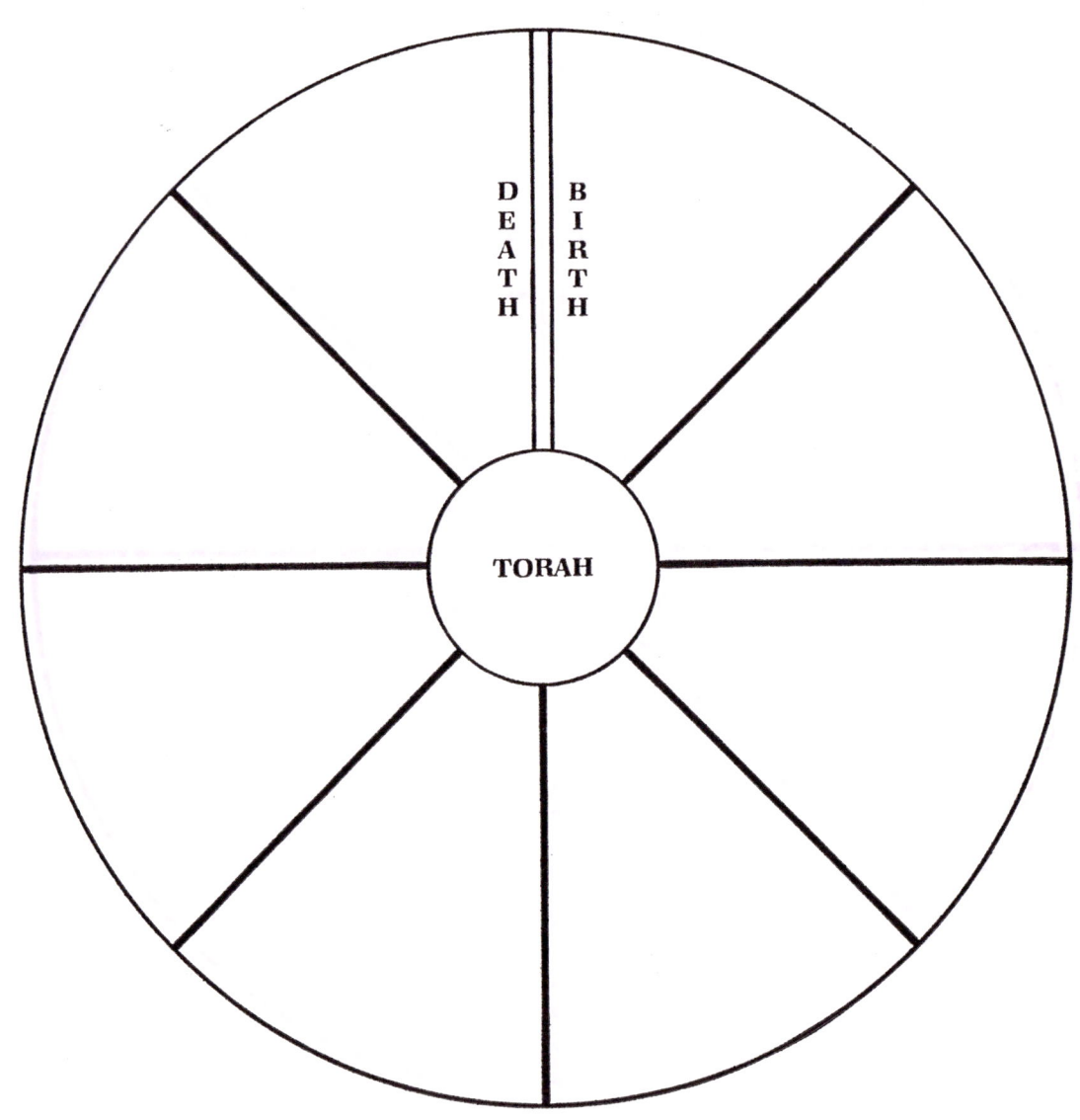

MASTER #13
Basic Judaism for Young People
Volume 2: Torah   NAME _____

A famous song says "The land of Israel without the Torah is like a body without a soul." Think of more comparisons and then fill in the blanks on the chart.

The land of Israel without the Torah is like ...

a day	without	sunshine
a fish	without	_____
a guitar	without	_____
_____	without	hamburgers
_____	without	_____
_____	without	_____
_____	without	_____

Use the space below to illustrate at least one of your comparisons.

MASTER #13
Basic Judaism for Young People
Volume 2: Torah

NAME _____

A famous song says "The land of Israel without the Torah is like a body without a soul." Think of more comparisons and then fill in the blanks on the chart.

The land of Israel without the Torah is like …

a day _____ without sunshine _____

a fish _____ without _____

a guitar _____ without _____

_____ without hamburgers _____

_____ without _____

_____ without _____

_____ without _____

Use the space below to illustrate at least one of your comparisons.

MASTER #13
Basic Judaism for Young People
Volume 2: Torah   NAME _____

A famous song says "The land of Israel without the Torah is like a body without a soul." Think of more comparisons and then fill in the blanks on the chart.

The land of Israel without the Torah is like ...

a day	without	sunshine
a fish	without	_____
a guitar	without	_____
_____	without	hamburgers
_____	without	_____
_____	without	_____
_____	without	_____

Use the space below to illustrate at least one of your comparisons.

MASTER #14
Basic Judaism for Young People
Volume 2: Torah   NAME _____

Use the words listed below to fill in the blanks in the following paragraph.

200 C.E.	Babylonian	Mishnah
500 C.E.	Gemara	Palestinian
Aggadah	Halachah	Talmud
Babylonia	Jerusalem	

The Talmud is a collection of legal writings known as **Halachah** and other writings known as **Aggadah**. The first part of the Talmud to be written was the **Mishnah**; it was compiled by Yehudah HaNasi around the year **200 C.E.** Commentaries on this work were later collected as the **Gemara**. Some commentaries were written by rabbis in Israel: their interpretations make up part of the **Jerusalem** Talmud, which is also called the **Palestinian** Talmud. Other commentaries were written by rabbis at academies in **Babylonia**: their interpretations form part of the Babylonian **Talmud**. Each Talmud is many times larger than the Bible, but the **Babylonian** Talmud is by far the larger of the two Talmuds. All work on the Talmud was completed by the year **500 C.E.**

MASTER #14
Basic Judaism for Young People
Volume 2: Torah

NAME _____

Use the words listed below to fill in the blanks in the following paragraph.

200 C.E.	Babylonian	Mishnah
500 C.E.	Gemara	Palestinian
Aggadah	Halachah	Talmud
Babylonia	Jerusalem	

The Talmud is a collection of legal writings known as _____ and other writings known as _____. The first part of the Talmud to be written was the _____; it was compiled by Yehudah HaNasi around the year _____. Commentaries on this work were later collected as the _____. Some commentaries were written by rabbis in Israel; their interpretations make up part of the _____ Talmud, which is also called the _____ Talmud. Other commentaries were written by rabbis at academies in _____; their interpretations form part of the Babylonian _____. Each Talmud is many times larger than the Bible, but the _____ Talmud is by far the larger of the two Talmuds. All work on the Talmud was completed by the year _____.

EASTER #18
Basic Judaism for Young People
Volume 2: Torah   NAME_____

Use the words listed below to fill in the blanks in the following paragraph.

200 C.E.   Babylonian   Mishnah
500 C.E.   Gemara   Palestinian
Aggadah;   Halachah   Talmud
Babylonia   Jerusalem

The Talmud is a collection of legal rulings known as _____ and other writings known as _____. The first part of the Talmud to be written was the _____. It was compiled by Yehudah HaNasi around the year _____. Commentaries on this work were later collected as the _____. Some commentaries were written by rabbis in _____. Interpretations make up part of the _____ Talmud which is also called the _____ Talmud. Other commentaries were written by rabbis at academies in _____. Their interpretations form part of the Babylonian _____. Each Talmud is many times larger than the Bible, but the _____ Talmud is by far the larger of the two Talmuds. All work on the Talmud was complete by the year _____.

MASTER #14
Basic Judaism for Young People
Volume 2: Torah   NAME _____

Use the words listed below to fill in the blanks in the following paragraph.

200 C.E.	Babylonian	Mishnah
500 C.E.	Gemara	Palestinian
Aggadah	Halachah	Talmud
Babylonia	Jerusalem	

The Talmud is a collection of legal writings known as _____ and other writings known as _____. The first part of the Talmud to be written was the _____; it was compiled by Yehudah HaNasi around the year _____. Commentaries on this work were later collected as the _____. Some commentaries were written by rabbis in Israel: their interpretations make up part of the _____ Talmud, which is also called the _____ Talmud. Other commentaries were written by rabbis at academies in _____: their interpretations form part of the Babylonian _____. Each Talmud is many times larger than the Bible, but the _____ Talmud is by far the larger of the two Talmuds. All work on the Talmud was completed by the year _____.

MASTER #15
Basic Judaism for Young People
Volume 2: Torah   NAME _____

Decorate this certificate with symbols that indicate some of the things you've learned this year. When you're finished decorating, cut out the certificate and have your teacher sign it.

This certificate shows that

_____

has satisfactorily performed
the Mitzvah of

תַּלְמוּד תּוֹרָה

DATE _____   TEACHER _____

MASTER #15
Basic Judaism for Young People
Volume 2: Torah

NAME _____

Decorate this certificate with symbols that indicate some of the things you've learned this year. When you're finished decorating, cut out the certificate and have your teacher sign it.

This certificate shows that

_____

has satisfactorily performed
the Mitzvah of

תלמוד תורה

DATE _____ TEACHER _____

MASTER #15
Basic Judaism for Young People
Volume 1: Torah   NAME _____

Decorate this certificate with symbols that indicate some of the things you've learned this year. When you're finished decorating, cut out the certificate and have your teacher sign it.

This certificate shows that

_____

has satisfactorily performed

the mitzvah of

_____   _____
 DATE   TEACHER

MASTER #15
Basic Judaism for Young People
Volume 2: Torah

NAME _____

Decorate this certificate with symbols that indicate some of the things you've learned this year. When you're finished decorating, cut out the certificate and have your teacher sign it.

This certificate shows that

_____

has satisfactorily performed the Mitzvah of

DATE _____   TEACHER _____

MASTER #16A
Basic Judaism for Young People
Volume 2: Torah   NAME _____

Lesson Planning for *Basic Judaism for Young People*

THE CONCEPT: _____
A one-sentence definition:

Relation to the literal English translation:

    Similarities:

    Differences:

Features of the concept highlighted in the textbook:

Your own examples of the concept:

Performance Objectives: By the end of the lesson, students will be able to:

Expressive Outcomes: During the lesson, students will have the opportunity to:

MASTER #16A
Basic Judaism for Young People
Volume 2: Torah

NAME _____

Lesson Planning for Basic Judaism for Young People

THE CONCEPT: _____

A one-sentence definition:

Relation to the literal English translation:

Similarities:

Differences:

Features of the concept highlighted in the textbook:

Your own examples of the concept:

Performance Objectives: By the end of the lesson, students will be able to:

Expressive Outcomes: During the lesson, students will have the opportunity to:

MASTER #16A
Basic Judaism for Young People
Volume 2: Torah   NAME:

Lesson Planning for Basic Judaism for Young People

THE CONCEPT:
A one-sentence definition:

Relation to the literal English translation:

    Similarities:

    Differences:

Features of the concept highlighted in the textbook:

Your own examples of the concept:

Performance objective: by the end of this lesson, students will be able to:

Expressive Outcomes: during the lesson, students will have the opportunity to:

MASTER #16A
Basic Judaism for Young People
Volume 2: Torah   NAME _____

Lesson Planning for *Basic Judaism for Young People*

THE CONCEPT: _____
A one-sentence definition:

Relation to the literal English translation:

    Similarities:

    Differences:

Features of the concept highlighted in the textbook:

Your own examples of the concept:

Performance Objectives: By the end of the lesson, students will be able to:

Expressive Outcomes: During the lesson, students will have the opportunity to:

MASTER #16B
Lesson Planning Form—page 2

Beginning the Lesson:

Reading and comprehending the text:

    Special topics:

    Illustrations:

    Student Activity Book:

Major activities:

    Additional activities:

    Duplicating master:

Concluding the lesson:

    "Review It"

REACTIONS: What actually happened in class? What worked best? What didn't seem to work?

MASTER #16B
Lesson Planning Form—page 2

Beginning the Lesson:

Reading and comprehending the text:

Special topics:

Illustrations:

Student Activity Book:

Major activities:

Additional activities:

Duplicating master:

Concluding the lesson:

"Review It"

REACTIONS: What actually happened in class? What worked best? What didn't seem to work?

MASTER #16B
Lesson Planning Form – page 2

Beginning the lesson

Reading and comprehending the text

   Special topics:

   Illustrations:

   Student Activity Task:

Major activities:

   Additional activities

   Duplicating masters

Concluding the lesson

   "Review It"

REACTIONS: What actually happened in class? What worked and what didn't seem to work?

MASTER #16B
Lesson Planning Form—page 2

Beginning the Lesson:

Reading and comprehending the text:

   Special topics:

   Illustrations:

   Student Activity Book:

Major activities:

   Additional activities:

   Duplicating master:

Concluding the lesson:

   "Review It"

REACTIONS: What actually happened in class? What worked best? What didn't seem to work?